REFRACTIONS: SOLO

EDITED BY DONNA-MICHELLE ST. BERNARD AND
YVETTE NOLAN

PLAYWRIGHTS CANADA PRESS
TORONTO

Playwrights Canada Press
202-269 Richmond St. W., Toronto, ON M5V 1X1
416.703.0013 • info@playwrightscanada.com • www.playwrightscanada.com

First edition: March 2014
Printed and bound in Canada by Marquis Book Printing, Montreal
Cover and book design by Blake Sproule

LIBRARY AND ARCHIVES CANADA CATALOGUING IN PUBLICATION
Refractions : solo / edited by Yvette Nolan and Donna-Michelle St. Bernard.

ISBN 978-1-77091-247-2 (pbk.)

1. Monologues, Canadian (English). 2. Canadian drama (English)--21st
century. I. Nolan, Yvette, editor of compilation II. St. Bernard, Donna-
Michelle, editor of compilation

PS8309.M6R44 2014   C812'.04508   C2011-902675-9

We acknowledge the financial support of the Canada Council for the Arts,
the Ontario Arts Council (OAC)—an agency of the Government of Ontario,
which last year funded 1,681 individual artists and 1,125 organizations in
216 communities across Ontario for a total of $52.8 million—the Ontario
Media Development Corporation, and the Government of Canada through
the Canada Book Fund for our publishing activities.

CONTENTS

Donna-Michelle St. Bernard & Yvette Nolan • Introduction   v

RED

Marie Clements • *Tombs of the Vanishing Indian*   3
Anita Majumdar • *Fish Eyes* and *The Misfit*   5
Wanda R. Graham • *Kill Zone a love story*   13
Daniel Macdonald • *A History of Breathing*   17
Jason Maghanoy • *Throat*   20
nisha ahuja • *Cycle of a Sari*   28
Julie Tepperman • *YICHUD (Seclusion)*   34
Colleen Murphy • *The December Man (L'homme de décembre)*   37
David Copelin • *The Rabbi of Ragged Ass Road*   40
Chris Craddock • *The Incredible Speediness of Jamie Cavanaugh*   44
Michael P. Northey • *Cranked*   47
Anusree Roy • *Letters to my Grandma*   50
Judith Thompson • *Lion in the Streets*   54
Sky Gilbert • *Will the Real JT Leroy Please Stand Up?*   57

YELLOW

Tara Beagan • *Dreary and Izzy*   63

C.E. Gatchalian • *Falling in Time*   68

Diana Tso • *Red Snow*   73

Peter Anderson • *The Blue Horse*   77

Nina Arsenault • *The Silicone Diaries*   80

Gein Wong • *Hiding Words (for you)*   92

Thomas Morgan Jones • *Samuel and Susan*   95

ahdri zhina mandiela • *who knew grannie: a dub aria*   98

Michael Rubenfeld • *My Fellow Creatures*   102

Ravi Jain, Katrina Bugaj, Troels Hagen Findsen, and
Nicolas Billon • *I'm So Close...*   105

David S. Craig • *Napalm the Magnificent:
Dancing with the Dark*   108

Don Hannah • *While We're Young*   114

Keith Barker • *The Hours That Remain*   117

Erin Shields • *If We Were Birds*   120

Ned Dickens • *Seven*   123

BLUE

Dawn Dumont • *Fancydancer*   129

Lisa Codrington • *The Aftermath*   133

David Yee • *carried away on the crest of a wave*   143

Tawiah M'Carthy • *The Kente Cloth*   147

Aaron Bushkowsky • *Soulless*   150

Joan M. Kivanda • *Stori ya*   153

Waawaate Fobister • *Agokwe* 161

Jon Lachlan Stewart • *Big Shot* 164

Mansel Robinson • *Two Rooms* 168

Shahin Sayadi • *The Veil* 176

INTRODUCTION

Refraction, in physics, is the change of direction of a ray of light, or sound, or heat, as it passes through one medium to another. In that passage things are altered, or, more accurately, we perceive them differently. Sound bends and becomes more or less audible, heat increases, and light—*ah, light*—white light seemingly splits into separate colours. They were always there, we just couldn't see them from where we stood. Our prism has split our selections into three sections: red and yellow and blue.

Red. In the heat of the moment we reveal ourselves, as we did not know ourselves to be. We bubble over, we explode, and sometimes we shift just enough to see unexpected layers. Michael Northey's Stan, the unlikely hero in *Cranked*, looks up from rock bottom and is able to imagine himself rising above. These are times when transformation happens in an instant; sudden, startling, and irreversible, like things that can never be unsaid. Julie Tepperman's Malka in *YICHUD (Seclusion)* and Judith Thompson's Rhonda in *Lion in the Streets* are women who, when pushed just too far, speak their truths without thought of the consequences.

Yellow. In the light of cooling embers we turn inwards, seeking the warmth of our cores and the reflection afforded us in the moment, once removed from the spark. We sink into a self still soft enough to take an impression. Nina Arsenault's heroine in *The Silicone Diaries* has undergone a transformation of herself through surgery and hormones that make her a work-in-progress, and affords her a view of two worlds. David S. Craig's Napalm is court-ordered to deliver a performance that gives him the opportunity to expose himself and his audience at once. Tara Beagan's heroines Dreary and Izzy are still so close to the pain that has transformed them that the only way they can make sense of it is by speaking their realities.

Blue. Sometimes there is clarity—which is not necessarily the same as truth—in sifting through the ashes. We find ourselves after the conflagration outside or above. We are able to see past the edges of happening into the broader panorama that allows us to recognize patterns, to see a way forward, to see past ourselves. Some like Khanoom in Shahin Sayadi's *The Veil* use this wisdom to counsel the next generation in patience and forgiveness. Some like April in Dawn Dumont's *Fancydancer* teach us, heartbreakingly, from the other side, just how sweet is this life.

As the new writers become visible, tracing the footsteps of our theatrical elders, like Judith Thompson and Don Hannah, and following the paths of those who have gone on, as have David French and Carol Bolt, we the audience become sensitized to all the voices in the landscape. The monologues we have selected here are culled from plays, from whole worlds that have been created by an amazing number of writers from all over this land. Each writer brings all of his or her history to the creation of the new world, which is rooted in this world, this land recently named Canada.

This collection was born of the desire to address a number of perceived needs: to offer young actors a banquet of possible monologues that may well reflect their realities more accurately, and therefore give them a better chance to shine in their often frustrating pursuit of work; to introduce theatre lovers to a host of perhaps unfamiliar writers who are emerging from a diversity of communities; to illuminate the Canadian theatrical landscape in a new way. We found it illuminating that the greatest number of pieces fell into the Yellow section of the book, the reflective but not nostalgic. From where we now stand it would appear that we are less immediate, we Canadian playwrights; we check over our shoulders to remember from whence we came, and we use that knowledge to break a trail forward.

The world of Canadian theatre is in the process of refracting. It is not splitting, or splintering, but rather finally just beginning to offer us all a fuller vision.

—Donna-Michelle St. Bernard and Yvette Nolan

RED

Marie Clements is an award-winning Métis performer, playwright, and director whose work has been presented on stages across Canada, the United States, and Europe. She is the founder of urban ink productions, a Vancouver-based First Nations production company that creates, develops, and produces Aboriginal and multicultural works of theatre, dance, music, film, and video. Clements was invited to the prestigious Festival de Theatre des Ameriques in 2001 for *Urban Tattoo* and in 2002 for *Burning Vision*. In 2002, she worked in the writing department of the television series *Da Vinci's Inquest*. A fellowship award from the BC Film Commission enabled her to develop the film adaptation of her stage play, *The Unnatural and Accidental Women*. She is also a regular contributor on CBC Radio.

Tombs of the Vanishing Indian weaves together the political chaos of 1970s Los Angeles with the triangular story points of three Oklahoma Indian sisters who board a Greyhound bus with their mother and end up in three very different tunnels in LA.

Jessie is an idealist physician who is married to a medical colleague.

Tombs of the Vanishing Indian premiered at Buddies in Bad Times Theatre, Toronto, co-produced by Native Earth Performing Arts and red diva projects in March 2011.

• • •

JESSIE

I dreamed once I had a mother and she had me, and I had two sisters, and she had them, and we were on a bus, with a skinny grey dog on the side, and my younger sister barfed on the floor, and it smelled and my other sister buried her baby face in my mother's deep breast and drank like that river was hers. I dreamed once I had a mother and she had me and I had two sisters and she had them and we were on a bus with a skinny grey dog on the side, and we were travelling a long way to make a new story, and it was hot and my mother opened the bus window, and a beautiful stream of wind came over us and it blew my mother's black hair all over our round faces that laid on my mother's body like we owned her. She said, just then, "Look girls, look at those rocks." These three big boulders standing just so in the desert, staring just enough for us to recognize them. She said, "Jessie, look, don't you recognize them from home, look how they stand," and I said, "Yes, I think I do." She said, "Jessie, the rock family are following us to LA, to start a new life too." Such are the things memories are made of.

ANITA MAJUMDAR
FISH EYES AND THE MISFIT

A graduate of the National Theatre School of Canada, Anita Majumdar holds a degree in English, Theatre, and South Asian Languages from the University of British Columbia. She is a classically trained dancer in Kathak, but has also studied Bharatanatyam and Odissi. Her first written/performed solo show, *Fish Eyes*, has toured across Canada and internationally and is a part of a trilogy of solo shows aimed at following strong South Asian Canadian heroines who use dance to navigate their dilemmas. A second solo show, *The Misfit*, is based on the issues of patriarchy and "honour killing" and was developed through a workshop performance tour across Canada. Anita is currently developing the plays *Same Same But Different*, *Boys With Cars*, and *Let Me Borrow That Top*.

FISH EYES

Meena is a South Asian Canadian teenager forced into taking classical Indian dance lessons from the age of five, blaming them for getting in the way of her love for Buddy Cain, a popular high-school jock who she dreams of being with in Hindi cinema-style fantasies. Rather than socializing, Meena spends her weekends performing at various events organized by her dance teacher, Kalyani Aunty. When Meena discovers that Buddy is dating another popular girl, she takes her frustrations out on Kalyani Aunty and quits an upcoming dance competition in India. Hurt, Kalyani Aunty shuts Meena out and replaces her with an inferior dancer, Lalita. As Meena struggles to redefine herself she finds herself gravitating back to her dance life.

Meena is an open-hearted seventeen-year-old girl who dreams of love in Hindi cinema song/dance sequences and is slowly learning how important owning up to one's identity really is.

Premiered at Theatre Passe Muraille, Toronto, in October 2005.

• • •

MEENA

So Kalyani Aunty's pretty mad at me. I asked her what time we were gonna go for our regular trip to Little India, but she said she was too busy! Okay, she's never too busy, not for Little India! So I tried to make her laugh, or at least yell at me like she usually does, so in dance class everyone's doing this *(demonstrates dance move)*, while I'm doing this *(demonstrates different dance move)*, but I'm doing this! *(demonstrates different dance move)* But nothing! I don't even get why she's so mad at me since she found a replacement for me... Lalita!

LALITA! The best she could come up with was Lalita? Okay, I know what you're going to say, "Hey Meena, why do you care, you didn't want to do the stupid dance competition anyways?" But I'm thinking of the quality of the Nimbooda dance. I don't think it's realistic to choose LALITA to do this top-notch dance competition when Lalita's getting married! Yeah, I thought it was pretty unbelievable too, but Lalita's engaged to our really hot tabla drummer, Sid? So? How's Lalita gonna focus on making the Nimbooda dance really, really good when she's got this Summer of Lalita and Sid wedding to think about?

So I thought I could just concentrate on school. Like, no dance, just school. But then our stupid dance got picked for the stupid school assembly. Remember gym class, the dance ensemble?

And Candice… Candice Paskas is all *like (uses an Indian dance hand gesture),* "Hey guys, I came up with some new moves. It's like 'Indian dance'?"

Indian? Hello?! I think I might just happen to know a little something about Indian dance!

And then Candice—Candice Paskas—is all like, "Hey guys, John Travolta did this one in *Pulp Fiction.* It's like Aquarius, like the Fish Eyes move!"

I'll show you FISH EYES! It's actually called Kartarimukha *(demonstrates the hand gesture).* It's the fourth mudra in a series of single hand gestures used to storytell in pure classical dance. I mean, let's have a little give and take here! First she steals my Buddy, my Grad 2006 date, my "Summer of Meena and Buddy," and then she wants to steal my dance too?

Beat. MEENA *collects herself.*

But then I went home and I started to think about how to make the dance good, well as good as it can be. And I came back like really excited because there's this problem spot in the dance that no one else could figure out, but I actually suggested doing a spin where we all do this!

MEENA *does a dance spin.*

But Candice is all like, "Um, I don't think they do that in Indian dance."

But then Candice's friends, who are usually like her "Yes Men," right? They said that they never thought I could dance like that. So I showed them some more stuff, like easy stuff, stuff I've been doing since I was really little, and they just ate it up! And the best part was? Candice Paskas couldn't say anything because she was the odd one out!

THE MISFIT

Naznin (Naz) is a respected, Canadian-born Kathak dancer with a dark past. After running off with an Indian hotel steward/aspiring pop singer (Lucky Punjabi), Naznin is disowned and abandoned in India by her parents all in the name of "honour."

In India she finds asylum as a choreographer for a dance troupe that performs classical Indian dances to English MTV pop music at wedding receptions. The company is run by a village matriarch named Gustakhi who loves Naz for her skills and for her ability to make the company a lot of money, but when she finds out that Naz has been ostracized by her family for running away with Lucky Punjabi, who was subsequently killed by his own village, Gustakhi is livid.

Gustakhi is a 48–56-year-old woman who assumes the role of "mother" readily. She is a shrewd and quick-witted businesswoman who has a great respect for money and public face, but treats life's injustices as very matter-of-fact.

Premiered at Theatre Passe Muraille, Toronto, in October 2008.

• • •

GUSTAKHI

Naznin, you're very smart, huh? So sharp. You have everyone
wrapped around your finger, taking sides and all... Tell me, has
the saliva on your body dried from when that toilet brush of a boyfriend licked there? Huh, let a girl go to college. Little knowledge
is dangerous. They come back and forget that this is how it will
always be! Lucky's mother, with a son that old, must have matched
his marriage up with good girl. And with one "jhetah," you took
it all away. This is what happens when you're raised abroad. What
kind of whore jumps into a bed slot warmed for another woman?

You don't talk about my daughter! What my daughter did to my
family...

No. I shouldn't have to explain it. If you were raised right, you would
know. If you had any concept of honour... *(beat)* My son's engage-
ment day. My daughter gallivants in, announcing, informing me in
front of everyone, that she too will be getting married... to some
boot-polish caste boy she met at college. Bride's family cancels marriage with my son. Good dowry that we needed? Gone. Any chance
of anyone wanting to marry into my family? Gone. We needed clean
slate for my son. So I told him, "You go take your late daddy's gun,
and take your sister to the field." When they brought their bodies?
Telling me that it was both murder and suicide? Can you tell me you
know what it is to see your own blood spilled in dirt? How it is to
have the blood in your veins ache and scream at same time? I saw

all that spilled blood and I ran to my kitchen and I got bottles and I filled them with all the blood I could squeeze and what I couldn't get, I licked with my mouth. You can't understand that, can you? That's what you do with your own blood. You keep it to yourself.

Wanda R. Graham is an award-winning actress and writer for stage, radio, and screen. She has a B.A. in Acting from Dalhousie University in Halifax and an M.F.A. in Playwriting from York University. She lives in a small fishing village in Nova Scotia.

Ray Warden may have tried to commit suicide. He may have been the only innocent soldier in the "kill zone" that night. Three things are certain: he has seen horrible things; he has done horrible things; he will have no public trial. His mother will always wonder what happened to the good soldier who put on the uniform for us.

Kill Zone a love story premiered in Halifax, Nova Scotia, presented by Heat Theatre in June 2013

• • •

RAY

Eight guys kneel bare-chested in'a pool'a mud,
might as well call it the colour of blood.
"Shove it in!" Sarge yells.
Dip the tip of my nose into the cold puddle.
Sarge's boot appears an inch from my right eye.
"I saa-id shove it in!" Toe of his boot presses
my head. Look over at Snoop, Grey, Shortie.

Sarge taps. My face sinks in'a muck.
Holds it, "Ah-whan an'a tooooo an'a tharrreeeah…"
Sarge is right proud of where he crawled up from—
sewer pipe in Nutbar Hotel.
"Y'not in the land a'unconditional love.
No one even likes you here."
He releases the pressure.
"At ease, excellent balls'a excrement."

Pull our faces out, pissed as hell,
slidin, bumpin, tryin'a see, tryin'a get
out of that mud.

Rug, one of the black guys, is naked,
tied to a tree. Covered in dried mud.
We learn later it's his own excrement.
"Nigger" slashed in white 'cross his

chest. Struggle to get to him through
the goo. Gonna rescue him. Least mess
up the nasty "N" word.

Guys are laughin. Rug's laughin.
Pretty—white teeth, half-naked, covered in mud.
Love my wife, ya, but never feel nuthin like this
confusion'a muck'n country 'n death.
Do anything for these mothers.
Same as they'd do for me. Stand 'ere, hand scratchin,
balls swellin alla way to my eye sockets ready t'explode
in deep appreciation'a all'a see.

Gigglin. Let Rug hang there, crucified
on the nasty "N" word. Y' goin through what
y'got to go through. "Here for ya, man, but not here
for ya. Catch my drift."

Dude makin a video has a hard time stayin clean.
Slidin round tight'n loosey-goosey
Suddenly in love with ourselves... we get it.
A'good ones do. "Got nothin but each other.
No more Ray. Call me Shit-for-Brains Homo Queen
Injun Nigger Suckhole Fuck-face-Fifi White Bread.
Pull out my nails waterboard me run current through
my balls, shove hot stones up my ass. Body parts,
excrement, eat'em warm for breakfast!"
Show my teeth to the camera. Elite Fighting Force,
the Airborne's emergin from this sludge.

Gimme m'Regimental coin, m'Airborne Tattoo!
My shield of love! Take a bullet for anyone wearin
these!

Askin what the heck's a military for? Us.
We make a'country proud! M'flag. M'guys.
M'wife, wherever she is! NOBODY dies on m'watch!
Slop like seals in'a mud teaches me how to fly!

Camera dude's laughin hard. Sarge done his job.
He knows he got us right. "Shove it in!
Eeeex-cellent balls of Excrement." No more choice.
Laying it down for y'brother like it's Normandy.
A split second and we're on our bellies, burying our
faces
the fastest and the deepest in'at loveliest'a
country mud. Rollie smiles'at smile all'a
way down, "No price too high for this kind'a GLORY!"

As a playwright Daniel Macdonald's plays include *Pageant*, *MacGregor's Hard Ice Cream and Gas*, *Velocity*, *Johnny Zed! The Musical!*, *Radiant Boy*, *Mercy*, and *A History of Breathing*, which was recently shortlisted for the Carol Bolt Award. He has also collaborated with students on several full-length plays for high schools. His plays have been produced and workshopped across Canada and the US. As a director his work has included *[title of show]*, *Eurydice*, *Mr. Marmalade*, and *The Unseen*. He is a two-time recipient of the City of Regina Writing Award and a recipient of the Enbridge playRites Award. He has an M.Ed and an M.F.A. (directing) and teaches high school and university classes. Recently he devised a new work with students to take to the Edinburgh Fringe Festival.

In a post-apocalyptic world, a great flood has claimed the land and many of its people. Two boats float aimlessly on an ocean that conceals the remains of civilization and history. One boat carries a father and daughter, the last survivors of an unspeakable catastrophe; the other carries the only hope for a new beginning.

Kai, 19, is neither a man nor a boy. He wants to win but has only the smallest notion of what this means—mainly to defeat the enemy—an enemy that does not exist. The "boy" in him will buy into that which brings the man in him the most power.

Developed at the Sage Hill Writing Experience's summer colony in 2008 and workshopped at the Saskatchewan Playwrights Centre's 2010 Spring Festival of New Plays, *A History of Breathing* was produced by Persephone Theatre in Saskatoon in 2012.

● ● ●

Dry land. A new kind of breathing. Panting. As though someone is out of breath. KAI appears, seated, eating fruit. A bloody machete sits by his side. KAI seems to be speaking off to someone just out of sight.

KAI

The first thing we did was create panic. Panic makes them stop thinking.

You make noise. You use large movements. You wave your machete around.

We didn't even have to speak. We just screamed and yelled.

And I tell you they panicked. Did they ever panic.

When they panicked they started thinking like survival.

This left them with only a few options of escape and we had thought of them before they had so we knew what they were going to do.

We knew what directions they were going to go and who they were going to take.

Mothers rarely leave behind children and so they go slow.

The girls go faster. Unless they have a baby.

We didn't kill them first. We stopped them.

There were about thirty of us. Me and maybe ten more boys and then some men.

We hit at the legs or ankles or shoulders, right at the neck. They fall quickly.

We killed as many men as we could find and then we took the boys.

We took the boys and brought them together and then we put one boy in front of another boy with a machete or a club and said, "Kill that other boy or I will kill you! Right now!"

We screamed it fast over and over so they didn't have time to think. One of us said, "Kill that boy or I will kill your sister. You see your little sister lying on the ground screaming? Kill that boy right now or I will chop your little sister in half!" So the boy killed the other boy. He cried and screamed the whole time he did it. Once he did that, he would do anything.

They would go anywhere. He'd seen it all. He'd done it all. He didn't care.

BOBO appears. He is no more than thirteen. He carries a handful of fruit, which he sets down. He does not sit. He holds a bloody machete.

Is that your story, Bobo? Is that what they did to you?

BOBO looks at KAI but does not respond.

We have to keep moving. See those walls up there? On the hill? That's where we should go. It'll be away from the water.

KAI and BOBO disappear.

Jason Maghanoy is a professional playwright, a graduate of the National Theatre School of Canada, a former member of the Banff Playwrights Colony, and a finalist for the 2011 Lila Acheson Wallace American Playwriting Fellowship at Juilliard. He has been a member of the Tarragon Playwrights Unit, Playwright-In-Residence at Cahoots Theatre Company, and most recently, Playwright-In-Residence at Theatre Passe Muraille. He has received grants for his work from the Toronto Arts Council, the Ontario Arts Council, and the Canada Council for the Arts, and his plays have been professionally produced in Edmonton, Toronto, Montreal, and Japan. Jason's work has also been featured as part of the Montreal Fringe Festival, the Toronto Fringe Festival, the Wildside Theatre Festival, the Next Stage Theatre Festival, and the SummerWorks Performance Festival. His plays *Gas* and *Dust* were published by Scirocco Drama, and his play *The Corner* was published in *Canadian Theatre Review*. *Throat* received second place in the 2010 Uprising National Playwriting Competition presented by Downstage Theatre and the Consortium for Peace Studies at the University of Calgary. For more information on his work please visit http://jsquaredtheatre.blogspot.ca.

A life-changing storm. A displaced community. *Throat* follows three friends who start a business cleaning up the government-sanctioned trailer park they live in. Their goal: to raise money to either buy back their old lives or live a better one. *Throat* is a play about those who have been displaced and how they seek to again find a place for themselves within society.

In a series of monologues over the course of the play, Teresa goes back to look at her old house in the city. She misses the house. She wants to go back to it. In this scene, Teresa watches a woman hang laundry in the backyard. This woman lives there now. Teresa is amazed by the beauty of the act. The simplicity. The purity of it all. As Teresa watches, her partner Trevor stalks a dying dog in the "Village," looking to clean it up after it dies.

Throat was developed at Cahoots Theatre Company as the playwright-in-residence, and it premiered in a staged reading at the 2010 CrossCurrents New Play Festival at Factory Theatre, Toronto.

CHOKE

TERESA *is in the city, standing by her old house. She watches a woman in the backyard as she hangs laundry on a wire. Whites. Colours. Blowing in the wind.*

TREVOR *follows the wheezing dog with the bone in its throat. The dog stumbles and lies down on the ground.*

TERESA

I do that sometimes… watch her hang clothes on the line. Watch her make her own little rainbow. They got nice clothes. Ain't seen a single hole in any of them. She takes good care, she does, just, workin and foldin and makin that rainbow.

TREVOR stands over the dog, watches it struggle to breathe.

It's so… nice to see I guess. The sunlight just makes the whites glow all hot, clothes gonna smell like the city, like home, and I watch the clothes blow in the wind like wings, like wings on this giant bird that can fly anywhere, sit on top of the highest mountain and watch all of us…

Beat.

When we go back… me and my mama are gonna do that too… create a rainbow… hang all them sundresses she gonna wear for all her photo shoots and we gonna watch that bird we create, watch it just grow and grow and grow like a beanstalk to Heaven. Bird's head in the clouds, bird's head beside God… watching us.

Them hoping that we can be good to each other.

That we can love each other.

That we make each other safe.

TREVOR slams his foot on the dog's neck.

TERESA smiles.

Black.

HOLD

TERESA *stands alone, staring at her old house.*

TERESA

The lights are off… and she sittin in the dark and I ask her to turn the lights on and she say that her eye red, she don't want me to see her with a red eye and I think that's the stupidest shit I ever heard… so I turn on the light and…

My mama was cryin. So bad. Tears make her look so beautiful you know? I just look at her and she make me want to strangle a bird.

She went to deliver something… for her business… over on Southside… and some motherfucker rob her… steal her shit and punch her in the eye.

I hold my mama's face. I want to take her tears and shove them back into her fuckin eyes. WHO THE FUCK WANT TO HURT A BUSINESS-WOMAN LIKE THAT?

I hold my mama and I tell her that we gonna leave this place, that I'm gonna buy our old house back and she look at me like I'm a crazy person and she say "people live there" and I say "FUCK THOSE PEOPLE… I got money. I work damn hard and I'm gonna take that money and put it at they feet, what are they gonna say to that? They gonna say no to all that money at their feet? Believe me, Mama, believe me, they gonna leave, they gonna go, they good people they'll understand, they gonna go, I'm gonna make them go I'm gonna...

I'm gonna buy it back."

TERESA *walks toward the house.*

I go to the house. And I wait I... sit on my front yard again. Sit where I used to sit with my dad, when we name our dandelion seed children and let them fly away. I lie on my back and watch the sky and I swear I see God in the clouds lookin at me laughin and I say, "I wanna laugh too! Joy just run though me like a current, make my hair stand up, brother, make me look like a motherfuckin clown!"

I turn on my side, take out a knife, write on the driveway a poem that I dreamed:

"I'm gonna swallow you. And I'm gonna grow. Grow so big that ain't nothing gonna be able to hurt me. I be a giant with skin that don't bleed. But you can cut me and feed on the shit I leak! Come and feed on me! I'm gonna take care of you. I'm gonna help you live.

I'm gonna be your home."

That'd be so crazy, eatin my house, house stick out of my stomach like a—

Suddenly, a harsh light.

TERESA *rises. She is looking at someone.*

(nervous) I'm sorry I just… I wanted to sit here and… I want to…
I want to—

Silence.

The other person is saying something to her.

(vicious) How about I call the cops on you, MOTHER—

• • •

TERESA *stands alone. She knocks on a door. The door opens.*

How are you, sir? My name is Teresa and…

I love the lights. Them white lights at the front of the house? Look
like little stars in they own universe, you know? I used to always
want to do that, reach up and grab a star, hold that shit in my hands,
even if my hands meltin because… that so rare… holding a star like
that… only God do stuff like that.

It's beautiful. Thank you for doing it.

I used to live here. This used to be my house. *It's true.*

We proud cause back then? We got the only tree on the block. My
mama plant it even though there be a bylaw against it.

When the storm come that tree fly away, shit get blown into my room.

So stupid having that tree.

(smiling) The bylaw was right.

Now all you got are them dandelions instead! Them fools come back home!

Like I knew they would.

   Beat.

When I was a little girl I used to keep my dead dog Alabama in a cooler in the backyard. Daddy say we ain't allowed to bury him because we may burst a gas pipe or some shit like that underground so we never dig.

Is Alabama still there? That blood drawing in the kitchen? That his blood, that shit still there?

   Silence.

I'm here because... I would like to offer you some money... so that I can have my house back... I have a business, cleaning up the village I live at and it's a lot of money, it's $8,000... and I'd like to give it to you, if you'd allow me back into my—

This is everything I work for.

Beat.

(hard) I live in Renaissance Village. Not the best place. Dark. Feel like the entire place dying of AIDS or something.

I'm sick of it.

And I want you to take this money, take this money and get out, just… give me my house back and IT'S NOT FAIR, THIS MY HOME, YOU LIVIN IN MY, GO, GO, GO, YOU CAN GO AND CALL THE FUCKIN COPS AND I WILL FUCKIN EAT THOSE MOTHERFUCKERS, PLEASE, PLEASE, DON'T, DON'T, PLEASE, YOU ARE NOT GONNA CLOSE THE MOTHERFUCKIN DOOR ON ME, NO, NO, YOU ARE NOT GONNA—

A flash of light… the faint sound of a gunshot.

Silence.

At night… in the Village… you walk around and you think you see God standing at every corner of the park. Man looks like he's crying all the time.

Everyone cryin. Everything so sad.

Silence.

It's just… so hard to show mercy.

Slow fade to black.

nisha ahuja, actor, writer, physical theatre and voice-over artist, singer/songwriter, and educator, has performed and created classical, contemporary, and original work across Canada, the Netherlands, and India. nisha was recently an actor with the National Arts Centre Resident Acting Company and toured her one-woman shows, *Yoga Cannibal* and *Un-settling*, across Canada and the province of Ontario. She is currently developing *The Besetting of Reena Virk* with Subtle Vigilance Collective, and is a core member of the R3 (Roots Rhythm Resistance) artists' collective. Some collaborations include Native Earth Performing Arts, Cahoots Theatre Company, New Harlem Productions, Buddies in Bad Times Theatre, the Canadian Stage Company, Factory Theatre, Theatre Direct, Carousel Players, Concerned for Working Children/Common Plants (Karnataka, India), the National Centre for Inclusion (Mumbai, India), Caravan Stage Tall Ship Theatre, the Ontario Council for International Cooperation's Just Theatre, Diaspora Dialogues, Salamander Theatre, and many independent theatre companies and community organizations. nisha graduated from York University with Specialized Honours in Theatre/Creative Ensemble and a Minor in International Development, and shares Yogic and Vedic energy medicine.

Partitioned from land and love in Sindh, Rani travelled to present-day India, and eventually to Turtle Island (North America),

also Partitioned Indigenous land. After her passing, Rani's ashes
are taken from her granddaughter, Asha, who calls Rani into her
dreams for answers on how to move forward after this interrupted
ritual. In the cosmos with grandmothers from other places and
times, Rani roots into ancestral wisdom and her life during the
Partition and Independence of South Asia all the while longing for
her love, Farah.

Rani tells Asha about demonstrating for South Asia's independence from the British Raj by weaving khadi saris with other
women, including Farah. In this monologue, Rani tells Asha about
the journey she took in leaving her homeland and Farah.

Received a public reading at the Canadian Stage Festival of New
Ideas and Creation in 2009, development support through Diaspora
Dialogues, a workshop performance at Patio Taller in Puerto Rico,
and is currently in development.

• • •

RANI

Why can't we just move to the Hindu colony? It's not so far.

We can stay there with people we know.

(as her husband) We can't trust the people we know.

(as herself) Yusef and Farah? Yusef and Farah who eat prashad
(translation from Hindi: blessed food from temple) with us every
full moon, even if it's after their Jummah prayer. Yusef and Farah

who light diyas *(translation: small clay candles)* at their house on Diwali and give you mithai *(translation: sweets)* on Eid. Yusef, who will always lose when he plays rummy with you, but who will always say yes when you ask him for a round. Farah, who has been, been like, like another sister to me. Both who have joined with us to show the Brits they aren't allowed to be here anymore. The ferengis *(translation: a derogatory term for foreigners)* need to leave, not us.

(as husband) Soon we'll be the ferengis in our own land, if we don't.

(as herself) That morning, packing what I can, we each carry a bundle. One of our weaving women, our weaving sister, and her family are to meet us at the station. Farah's sister is to arrive on the train at five a.m. Our train leaves at five thirty. Farah will welcome her blood sister to a new home, as I will leave her for who knows how long.

We all walk to the station together.

He won't even look at Yusef and Farah. I am stuck in the middle like a border defining their territories.

Five a.m.

Farah's sister's train hasn't arrived. Late as usual. Our weaving sister approaches the station with Jija ji, my brother-in-law, and my little niece, all carrying a bundle each. Looking into their eyes, even though bloodlines are blurred, we know we are lucky to have each other.

Five thirty a.m.

Not a train in sight, just waiting.

Five forty a.m.

Our train slowly pulls up to the platform, but people immediately push forward to start boarding. My sister waves to show me she and her family are safely boarding the car in front of mine.

Farah and I hold each other close, knowing this will likely be the last time we see each other. My stomach cries. The men awkwardly look away.

They turn back, trying to pull us apart, but are stopped by each other's eyes, and they silently nod their solemn goodbyes as Farah and I let go of our embrace, without our husbands ever knowing what we shared.

Five forty-seven.

Farah's sister's train still hasn't arrived, but ours is finally ready for departure. The engine winding up before we get moving.

In the distance, slow metallic boxes huff toward us down the track. This is it. They would arrive, take our places in the towns we called home, and I suppose we would take theirs. Muslims and Hindus trading places across newly drawn boundaries.

Our train begins to slowly pull us away from the platform.

As Farah's sister's train approaches, joyous hands wave to loved ones from the cars. As the train draws closer the arms and hands that wave seem limp. Limp and piled on top of legs. Piled on top of each other. Piles and piles. Piles and piles of blood.

I turn to look back out the window. Farah's jaw falls and her knees hit the ground, and there is what feels like a sea of a thousand people between us. She can't see me. Then I can't see her. The sea of people gets thicker, then pounds on the sides of our train as we pull away from our homeland, land we will never see again.

Ten hours later.

On our train travelling through open plains, men. Many, many men. A mob with large knives, and rage engraved into their faces. Their people were slaughtered, so now we must be massacred too. They rush the train and try to pull the doors open. The men in our car barricade all the entrances. But my husband knows my sister, my weaving sister, is in the car in front of us. The car in front of us, the car in which my dear, strong sister sits with her daughter and husband, where my husband has gone to... the car in front of us, the car in front of us, which is not barricaded... The rush of men get in anywhere they can.

Hours of hovering close to the floor, I huddle beneath the seats.

Hours. Hours of not knowing.

We pull into the station of our new promised home. Our car, along with only one other, unloads onto the platform. The rest, the rest, including the car in front of us, the car that my sister travelled in, that my husband went to, have the same limp hands and feet we saw on the train when we left Sindh. The trains arrive in my old home and my new one stacked with death. In one day, Farah and I are parted from the most important people in our lives, the women in our lives. Parted in Partition. Parted Independence.

Another sea of people gush around us. My husband, my weaving sister, my brother-in-law, are nowhere, and yet everywhere. From behind the piles of piles of piles emerges the tiny, numb five-year-old face of my niece. My new daughter.

JULIE TEPPERMAN
YICHUD (SECLUSION)

Julie Tepperman is a Toronto-based playwright, actor, and educator. She is also the co-founding artistic director of Convergence Theatre (with Aaron Willis), creators of the hit plays *AutoShow*, *The Gladstone Variations*, and *YICHUD (Seclusion)*. Writing credits include: *ROSY* (for *AutoShow*), *I Grow Old* (for *The Gladstone Variations;* Dora nomination, one of *NOW Magazine*'s Top Ten Toronto Productions of the Decade), and *The Father* (a re-imagining of the August Strindberg play) commissioned by the Winnipeg Jewish Theatre as part of the Manitoba Theatre Centre's 2011 Master Playwright Festival.

Set in Toronto's Orthodox Jewish community, *YICHUD (Seclusion)* centres on the arranged marriage of Rachel Blitzer and Chaim Berman, exploring issues of marriage, love, sex, respect, honour, and duty.

After twenty-nine years of marriage, Malka has asked Mordechai for a divorce. The arrangements have been made and the divorce will proceed the following week, but they have agreed to wait to tell their family after their daughter Rachel's wedding. Malka desperately wants to get through the day without Mordechai making a scene, but he corners her alone under the *chuppah* after the wedding ceremony, and insists that she listen to his new plan to save their marriage. When Morty presents her with a gift of red lacy panties (which are too small) and asks her to put them on for the reception, Malka has finally had enough.

Premiered at Theatre Passe Muraille, Toronto, in a producing partnership with Convergence Theatre in February 2010.

• • •

MALKA

I have sat here and I have listened to you go on and on about things that, *chas v'sholem*, I should be embarrassed to utter to another living soul. And since this little… has degenerated into such… filth *(She throws the panties at him on the word "filth.")* you will forgive me if I am no longer in control of what comes out of my mouth.

    Beat.

Do you want to know what sex was like with you, Mordechai? Do you really want to know? Do you? *(He remains silent.)* When you and I had sex, it was as if you were going to the bathroom on top of me. And as soon as your… urge was relieved, you would fall asleep and I was discarded, like a piece of toilet paper.

    Silence.

When I agreed to marry you, I thought, oh he's a good person, he's a kind person. He'll make a good father, he'll provide for his family. You do know you were not the first match the *shadchan* brought me. There were others, but none of them… I thought, if I said no to your proposal and then three, four months later I saw you walking down the street with some other girl on your arm, the thought of that made me cringe. I had never felt such jealousy before, such... longing... What did I know—I was nineteen years old. So I said yes! I snatched you up, like a *rugella* in a bakery, before anyone else could get a taste. And yes, Mordechai, you have been a good father, a loving father to our four girls, they adore you. But this... feeling has persisted.

Jealous of what? It's not as if you look at other women. You're not a scholar with your nose always buried in some book. Surely I'm not jealous of your work, you're home from the store when you say you'll be home... jealous of what?

At night, when I would undress in front of you and your eyes never left the television set... what, was I supposed to be jealous of the TV? Each month when I would come home from the *mikveh*, purified and ready for you, only to discover that you were asleep...

Beat.

Then one night it hit me. I had become jealous... of nothing. I realized if I could look at you, lie next to you, and feel nothing at all, then you would no longer be able to disappoint me, Mordechai.

MORDECHAI *tries to interrupt but she won't let him.*

You say this is a two-way street but for years I have been walking one way and you another. I am forty-eight years old, Morty, and I have nothing left. I am an empty hollow shell.

COLLEEN MURPHY
THE DECEMBER MAN (L'HOMME DE DÉCEMBRE)

Colleen Murphy was born in Rouyn-Noranda, Quebec, and grew up in northern Ontario. Her play *The December Man (L'homme de décembre)* won the 2007 Governor General's Literary Award for Drama, the 2008 Carol Bolt Award, and the 2006 Enbridge playRites Award. Other plays include *Pig Girl, Armstrong's War, The Goodnight Bird, Beating Heart Cadaver* (nominated for a 1999 Governor General's Literary Award and a Chalmers Award for Best New Play), *The Piper, Down in Adoration Falling,* and *All Other Destinations are Cancelled.* Colleen is also an award-winning filmmaker, showing in festivals around the world, and has been nominated for a total of eight Genie Awards.

In the aftermath of the 1989 Montreal Massacre, Benoît and Kathleen do everything they can to help their beloved son cope with his guilt and rage... but Jean's young life becomes unglued. Using humour and the humdrum of everyday life, the play intuitively moves backward in time to the fateful day when Jean, the only ray of hope in this working-class family, escaped the massacre.

A year after the massacre Jean is still battling nightmares. One night his screams wake his mother and he tells her about a special, reoccurring dream he has where he is cast as a hero.

Premiered at the Enbridge playRites Festival of New Canadian Plays at Alberta Theatre Projects in February 2007.

• • •

JEAN

Do you know what I dream about sometimes, Ma? I dream that no one died. *(a moment)* It's a special dream but it starts the same way— he comes in and says, "Everyone stop everything," but everybody ignores him until he fires at the ceiling. At first I think it's a scary joke... then he says, "Separate—girls on the left, guys on the right." No one even moves till he shouts, and then the guys, we go over to the right side where the door is. He waves the women to the back left corner. Then he says, "Okay—guys leave, women stay." There's nine women and about forty-five guys and two professors... so we leave the room and a few of us stand out in the hall... we hear the guy talking and a woman talking then bam bam bam... but in the special dream I... I run back into the classroom and he's standing there, his back to me, I could see the women bunched up against the wall, moaning and... ah... I was so scared 'cause I never open my mouth in class—even when I don't understand something I just sit there praying someone else will ask the question but suddenly I hear someone shout STOP. At first I think it's a professor who walked in behind me or a policeman but it's me, I'm shouting at the guy, and he swings around and fires and I veer to one side and I say PUT IT DOWN but he just keeps firing so I take a bullet in the leg, another in the side of my head, then calculate that the only way to stop the guy is tackle him—he's only about five-foot ten, skinny, maybe a hundred and fifty—so I jump him and his eyes open wide and he runs out of the room and I'm screaming to the guys out in hall to stop him... then... then I start sprouting extra arms so I start scooping up the wounded women until they're all in my arms and I run out and down the corridor, covered in blood, running behind him screaming YOU FUCKING COCKSUCKING MURDERING FUCK PIG SAVAGE—I don't know where all these extra arms are coming from, Ma, but I keep scooping up women who are wounded, lifting them, holding onto them for dear life until I can hardly move and I'm drowning in their blood but I stagger outside and get them to the ambulances in time and no one died, Ma... then I wake up. *(a moment)* That's what I most hate, Ma, that he was so angry and I was so afraid... I ran... I ran out of the classroom and I ran and ran, then I missed the bus and figured that was a sign for me to turn back but I was cold so I got on the metro at Côte-Sainte-Catherine and decided I'd just go one stop then get off at Plamondon and go back to the school, but I went right past Plamondon, past Namur, past De La Savane, and when I got off at Du Collège I automatically started walking down Ste. Croix. I kept telling myself to turn around turn around turn around but I was shaking and so I ran along Rue Hodge then turned onto Rue Petit and... *(begins to weep)* I left them all to die. *(a moment)* Ma? They're following me. The women... they're following me.

DAVID COPELIN
THE RABBI OF RAGGED ASS ROAD

David Copelin is a playwright, dramaturg, and translator. His play
Bella Donna won the New Play Award at the 2005 Toronto Fringe
Festival and was subsequently staged at the RCA Theatre in St.
John's and at Toronto's Berkeley Street Theatre. David's translation
of Alfred Jarry's *Ubu Roi* has been produced at the Shaw Festival,
Yale Repertory Theatre, and numerous universities. He is currently
working on two full-length original plays, *Let the River Answer* and
Winner Take Nothing, as well as translations of Carl Sternheim's
Citizen Schippel and *Tabula Rasa*, both with John Van Burek. David
is a member of the Playwrights Guild of Canada and the Dramatists
Guild of America. He is represented by Michael Petrasek at The
Talent House in Toronto.

When her husband dies in a mountain-climbing accident, Rabbi
Susan Brenner loses her faith and quits her Victoria congregation
in spectacular fashion. She flees to Yellowknife, where her younger
brother Barry is a lawyer for a diamond mine. Barry has fallen in
love with Jo, a Dogrib woman facing a major medical challenge.
Jo's survival depends on Susan, whose encounters with a native con
artist, a lovelorn skeleton, and the raven who flew out of Noah's Ark
complicate the reality she thought she knew.

The Rabbi of Ragged Ass Road was developed at ScriptLab in Toronto. Various drafts have received readings at Native Earth Performing Arts and the Miles Nadal Jewish Community Centre in Toronto, and at Magic Theatre in San Francisco.

• • •

SUSAN

Michael is dead. Michael, my husband. My soulmate, my *beshert*, the one God intended for me. Gone. Many of you have expressed your sympathy, done kind things, sat *shiva* with me. Grieved. I thank you all for your decency and good will. But it is not enough.

I have dreams. Of hands. Michael's hands. Soft, they were soft, I never did understand how they could be so soft when he did so much work outdoors. But they were. And gentle. When he first touched me I was ready to endure any pain, I just wanted him inside me, and he touched me and there wasn't any pain, just his hands, warm, stroking me so gently, making me unfold, making me joyful, making me crazy, and then we became one flesh and I have never been so sane.

Remember his eyes? Michael's eyes? They were sad, always. At first I thought *he* was sad, but he wasn't. He was happy, most of the time, but his eyes… He laughed and told me they were his grandma's eyes, and he didn't care how sad they looked, he loved his grandma, his *bubbe*. His eyes…

He was scared. When he knew for sure that he couldn't hold on any longer, when he had to let go and fall all that way, and he looked at me and I couldn't do anything but look back at him and watch him drop and his hands couldn't hold on and the rocks and the twigs snagged and broke them on his way down and it didn't matter how gentle they were, they were grasping hard at the air and his eyes kept looking into my eyes and I couldn't look away and I couldn't scream and I couldn't go with him and I couldn't save him and then he hit the big rock and broke. I heard him crack! And I am trapped by Michael's eyes, they're full of rage and terror and his hands are like gravel and everywhere is hell.

SUSAN starts to remove her vestments, slowly at first, then with increasing momentum.

God isn't love. God is cruelty. I can't be a rabbi any more. And you don't want a rabbi like me. Are you there, Adonai? Are you there, Holy One, Eternal One, ruler of the universe? Are you anywhere? My God, if you were silent during the Holocaust, why should you answer me now? For four thousand years you have lived in Jewish hearts. Well, no more free rent!

SUSAN opens a white box and removes a small Torah scroll. She whips off its sleeve and unrolls it a little, holding it up so the audience can see.

This was Michael's personal Torah, all that he had left of his father. He cherished it. Now it's mine. Look at it. Now. What God did to Michael, I do to God.

She sets the scroll on fire.

No, watch it burn! Any response up there? Hello? Show me, God!
Prove to me and to these your people that you exist! Kill me!

Nothing happens.

Kill me, too!

Nothing happens.

CHRIS CRADDOCK
THE INCREDIBLE SPEEDINESS OF JAMIE CAVANAUGH

Chris Craddock is an Edmonton-based actor, producer, and writer. His theatre work in Canada has been recognized with four Sterling Awards and two Dora Mavor Moore Awards, and his film *Turnbuckle* was nominated for two AMPIA Awards. He is the proud recipient of the Enbridge Emerging Artist award, the Centennial Medal for his contribution to the arts in Alberta, and the Alberta Book Award for his collection of plays for teens, *Naked at School*. His musical *BASH'd!* (co-written and performed with Nathan Cuckow) received a 2007 GLAAD media award.

Jamie Cavanaugh has a problem. She's different. Everyone says she's going too fast. But perhaps her speediness is not a problem; maybe it's a super power that she can use to defend her friend Max against the school bully, Rock. She's in more trouble than ever, and when everyone turns against her, her parents are at the end of their rope. Fortunately, help arrives when a school counsellor sends Jamie to a doctor and she is diagnosed as having attention deficit hyperactivity disorder (ADHD). Her parents begin to understand that Jamie has a learning disability, but the struggle to find the right combination of drugs to control it is anything but simple and that process tests Jamie's courage and strength of character to the limit.

Jamie is a fast-talking little girl at the end of her rope. Though bright and winning, at this point, her life, and her fantastical reason for all the problems in it, has fallen apart. She feels alienated and alone, and she can't talk her way out of it this time.

First produced by Roseneath Theatre in 2008 in Edmonton, Alberta.

● ● ●

JAMIE

Doing all of this for nothing. Isn't that the worst thing, when you try so hard for so long, all for nothing? I was still making my parents sad, Max wasn't my friend. He'd rather be friends with a bully who hurts people.

I went downstairs to get a glass of juice. It was the middle of the night, and I was completely awake and super thirsty, all because of these stupid pills. I was weirder than ever because of these drugs.

I was trying to be quiet. I opened the cupboard. I got a glass and… I dropped it!

Sound effect: SMASH!

There I go again. I'm exactly the same. I'm not a superhero. I'm a terrible kid that no one likes who makes her nice mom crazy. If I can't be a hero, I'll be the freak they say I am. I'll be a villain.

So I use my super speed and I make a whirlwind.

She opens the fridge and starts throwing the food and jars out onto the floor. She heaves a large jar through the kitchen window.

And the fridge door flies open and all the jars and the milk and the food flies out and the window breaks!

And then I run.

She starts to run in place. Sound effects: wind, increasing in intensity, zipping sounds as things whip past.

I run away from all these problems, from my angry friend and my stressed-out parents and being a big disappointment to everyone. I run from school and life and the principal and the teacher who makes jokes about me to the other kids. I run from the bullies and bad news and the doctors and the pills. And the world is blurring past me, and I run out of our city and across oceans and up buildings and onto the air.

And I run and run and run and run.

And when... I am out of breath... and I have to stop... and...

I see that I am just down the street.

I didn't get anywhere at all.

I'm not fast enough.

My mom and dad are walking down the street towards me. I can see that they're mad, but also, they're scared.

Michael P. Northey has acted in many theatre productions including *Glengarry Glen Ross*, *Mojo*, *The Overcoat*, *Problem Child*, *The Odd Couple*, and the one-man show *Samaritan*. Michael has also written a number of stage plays including *Reservations for Four*, *Rocket's Red Glare*, *A Dog Called Bitch*, *Reservations For Two*, *Stuck!*, *This Fringe Venue Is Now Being Held Hostage*, *This Fringe Venue Is Now Being Held Hostage… Again*, and *Ash Rizin*. His play *Cranked*, which was commissioned and produced by Green Thumb Theatre, won the 2007 Jessie Award for Best Original Script, toured Australia, New Zealand, Canada, and the US. Michael also works in film, television, and radio as an actor, writer, and voice-over artist. He is a graduate of Studio 58.

Stan, a.k.a definition, was a horror-film buff and a rising MC when it all crashed. As he preps for an upcoming competition without the crystal meth habit that dominated his previous life, his memories of the films, the meth highs, and the rush of music all collide as he struggles to recapture his life.

Premiered at Green Thumb Theatre, Vancouver, in October 2006.

MICHAEL P. NORTHEY ·

• • •

STAN

I remember once hearing my old man use the term "rock bottom."
He was referring to when he and my mom first got married and the
money wasn't rolling in so much and they ended up getting evicted.
Rock bottom? That ain't even close. I know rock bottom. Been there.
Lived there. My middle name's rock bottom.

Rock bottom is scratching at a piece of old chewed-up chewing gum
on the pavement 'cause you're pretty darn sure it's really a quarter.
It's smoking your own scabs because there's actually enough meth
in your skin to get you high. Rock bottom is... "Listen... Mom, I
swear I'll find out who did this. And when I do? I'm gonna kill 'em.
I'm serious! Hey... no... I ain't playin. These guys are toast. Why...
why are you looking at me like that? What? What, you think I did
it or something? You gotta be kidding me! Steal Pamela's birthday
presents! Steal the locket you gave her? You know I wouldn't do that.
You know that. What about you, Pam? You believe me, don't you?
Huh? You're my sister. Family doesn't steal from family. I know I
did it before. I know that. But that was different. This time I didn't...
What? Bleeding? Where? Oh... uh I musta... musta cut myself or...
Look, I told you I was clean and I am. I swear to... I don't do that...
I'm clean. No! Don't call Dad! Don't! Why are you dialing? I said
don't! Please! I'm clean! I'm clean! I'm clean!" Rock bottom? Shoot,
I hit rock bottom, grabbed a shovel, and kept on digging.

Okay look, I been thinking about all that you've been saying and well I mean that's hard 'cause you say a lot. I mean you kinda ramble on and on. No offence. I mean almost to an annoying level, really. But, well, I think I finally know why I did meth. Ready? Okay, well, I did meth so I could experience rapid weight loss and malnutrition. I did it to have intense paranoia and hallucinations. I wanted to encounter mood disturbances, rages, and violent behaviour, and undergo extreme delusions, and finally meet death due to brain hemorrhage or cardiovascular shock. Boo yah! Bet you're wondering where I came up with that, aren't ya? Aren't ya? It's on the poster right behind your desk. Woo! Eat it, Dinky! Eat it! Poisonous household cleaners and cough syrup. That's what floats my boat, Jackson! Wrap it up and tie it in a bow! I'll take it! Hey, what do you wanna bet I can get to that pen and stick it in your eye before you can stop me? Huh? What do you think?

Anusree Roy was born and raised in Calcutta, India, before moving with her family to Toronto. Her plays include *Pyaasa, Letters to my Grandma, Roshni*, and *Brothel #9*. She is the recipient of three Dora Mavor Moore Awards, the RBC Emerging Artist Award, the Carol Bolt Award, the Siminovitch Protege Prize, the K.M. Hunter Artist Award, and was nominated for the Governor General's Literary Award. She holds an MA from the University of Toronto's Graduate Centre for Study of Drama and is the co-artistic director of Theatre Jones Roy.

Letters to my Grandma weaves together the journeys of a grandmother and her granddaughter. On the day of her wedding, Malobee reads back through her grandmother's letters, revealing her grandmother's fight to survive in Second World War India and her own struggles to create a new life in present-day Toronto. In this monologue, Grandma is seen at age eighteen. She is a fighter, tremendously determined.

Premiered at Theatre Passe Muraille, Toronto, in March 2009, produced by Theatre Jones Roy.

This is a solo play, it was written and intended for a single actor to play all roles.

•••

This monologue takes place in 1947, Burma.

Grandma at eighteen is holding her shawl as her baby as she frantically runs for help.

GRANDMA

Bachao! Bachao! Kau ache! Aamar kache baby! Bachao! Shh...[1] someone will come for us. Shh. Stay calm. Ma is here. *(She spots a passerby.)* PLEASE! Please please. There was hatred in everyone's eyes. Everyone is dead... their eyes are dead. *(notices a passerby, runs towards them)* Dada,[2] dada, dada, where is everybody? I have a baby, only five hours old, dada, please help. Do you know where my family... No, dada, we are all Hindu. Our full blood is Hindu... not Muslim at all. What do you mean "Muslim Trucks"? They don't have Hindu trucks picking up Hindu people? Why not? But this is a Hindu area. Wait... wait... *(notices someone else, runs towards them)* Didi,[3] didi, didi, my husband has left me, didi... no... only a few hours old, didi. Do you know where the Basu family is hiding? Which ship? When did they leave? What... listen... come back... No they didn't. They couldn't have left. We will find them, shona.[4]

---

1   Save me! Save me! Is anyone here! I have a baby! Save me! Shhh...

2   Brother.

3   Sister.

4   Sweetheart.

You just stay alive... that's all you do. Ma will fix everything. Ma will be here. Always always always. Hai Thakur tumi dhekho... tumi![5]

Startled, she turns around to the sounds of a truck roaring by.

Eh wait wait! STOP THE TRUCK! Stop the tuck. Please, I have a baby... save us. Bahisab... bhaisab.[6] Mai Muslim hoo.[7] I am a Muslim. Allah Ki kassma.[8] I swear on our Allah. Yeh mera baccha hai.[9] I just gave birth, bhaisab. Please bhaisab... you will be able to fit us in your truck. No I won't! I will sit on the floor. If you want I will not even breathe in there. Look look... that woman that you have in there, she is not even Muslim. No, that one, the one with the little girl child... Allah ki kassam. She is the nurse that used to work in the womens' ward. No she is not! These Hindus are taking up our space. She is not Muslim... See... bhaisab, wouldn't you carry a Muslim and her baby so Allah blesses you? My family is very rich, you take me to the ship and my husband will give you money.

Get the nurse off. Get her off!

No no no, don't throw the child. Throw the mother. Throw her!

The woman is thrown off the Jeep. GRANDMA *spits on her.*

---

5 Dear God, you see us through, you!

6 An endearing term in Hindi used in reference to calling an unknown man brother.

7 I am Muslim.

8 I swear on Allah.

9 This is my child.

YOU ARE HINDU! What baby? See, these Hindus will come and make up stories. I don't know her. Allah ki kassam. Please, bhaishab, we are wasting time. The ship will leave soon and I have to find my husband so he can give you money.

She gets on the truck.

(She sits, speaking to the girl child.) Stop your crying. Your mother will be fine. Stop it.

Sudden pang of guilt. Beat. Looks around and speaks to the rest of people on the truck.

Are you all Muslim? Me neither. Will you pray with me for her? She was the Najma, the Muslim nurse who helped me deliver my baby.

She closes her eyes and prays.

JUDITH THOMPSON
LION IN THE STREETS

Judith Thompson is a two-time winner of the Governor General's Literary Award for *White Biting Dog* and *The Other Side of the Dark*. In 2006 she was invested as an Officer in the Order of Canada and in 2008 she was awarded the prestigious Susan Smith Blackburn Prize for her play *Palace of the End*. Judith is a professor of drama at the University of Guelph and lives with her husband and five children in Toronto.

The ghost of a murdered young girl flits through every scene of this dark drama. *Lion in the Streets* deals with those suffering from inner emotional turmoil. In this ensemble piece, the character of the ghost acts as a poignant reflection of the suffering of the other characters.

Lion in the Streets received its world première at the duMaurier Theatre Centre as part of the duMaurier World Stage Theatre Festival in Toronto in June 1990.

•••

RHONDA

LET MEEEEE TALLLLLK. LET ME TALK LET ME TALLLLLLLLLLLLK!! I feel... nailed to the wall by you, lady, nailed right to the fucking wall. I have to say and something else I have to say is that I think you are... are very... inconsiderate... of feelings! I brought up two kids on what I feed your kids, and they turned out just fine, are you telling me what I feed my kids isn't good enough for your kids? You know the funny thing is, Laura, you may be a bitch on wheels, but lookin at all the rest of you, Laura? At least you're honest you are. Youse others, what you're thinkin is... it really doesn't matter what they get at the daycare, the real learning is at home, that's where youse teach your kids to become—huh. Here I am saying "youse," I haven't said that since I was a kid! That's how flustered I am—at home you teach your kids... to be... higher kind of people, higher kind of people don't eat Kraft slices and tuna casserole, I've seen that kinda laugh in your voices, all of you, when you say, "Oh, they had *tuna casserole*." I seen, I have seen the roll in your eyes at the grace before meals, or the tidy-up song, or the stars we give out for citizen of the week, you think, oh well the kid is happy, well cared for, we can undo all that and we can make the kids high people like ourselves, better people, more better people than the poor little teacher who reads ROMANCE, yes, yes, JILL MATHINS, I saw you showin my book, my novel to RON there and Cathy and havin a big giggle, you think I didn't see that? You think the books you read are deeper more... higher, well it's the same story, don't you see that? What's makin me cry in my book is, when ya come right down to it, is exactly the same thing that's makin you cry in your book, oh yes, oh yes and I'll tell you something, I'll tell all of you I GREW UP ON THAT. I grew up on jelly doughnuts and butter tarts, and chocolate ice cream, and I happen to think they're a wonderful thing. I happen to agree with the mice and the cockroaches and the horses and birds that treats are a wonderful thing, you need treats, you need treats in this life, each bit of a treat can wipe out a nasty word, every bite of a jelly doughnut cleans out your soul, it is a gift from GOD, a wonderful gift from GOD and I for one... I for one... I... for... your eyes, eh? Your eyes are all the same colour and shape like a picture, a... freaky art picture all the same in a row like dark soldiers raisin your...

SKY GILBERT
WILL THE REAL JT LEROY PLEASE STAND UP?

Sky Gilbert is a writer, director, and drag queen extraordinaire. He was co-founder and artistic director of Buddies in Bad Times Theatre for eighteen years. He has received two Dora Mavor Moore Awards, Pauline McGibbon Award for theatre directing, the Margo Bindhardt Award, the Silver Ticket Award, and the ReLit Award (for his fourth novel *An English Gentleman*, 2004). Dr. Gilbert holds a University Research Chair in Creative Writing and Theatre Studies at the School of English and Theatre Studies at the University of Guelph.

Inspired by the important and timely issues raised by the real-life JT LeRoy hoax, a transgendered person named JT LeRoy comes to Scarsdale to visit a rich ex-rock musician who she suspects of being the real author of the books by JT LeRoy. The real JT confronts the writer and Amanda gives a spirited defence of herself as an artist who has the right to write. JT LeRoy has just confronted Amanda, threatening to expose the fact that Amanda is posing as a transgendered person, and that Amanda's books—which were supposedly based on the real-life experience of JT LeRoy—are a fraud.

Premiered at Buddies in Bad Times Theatre, Toronto, in April 2007.

• • •

AMANDA

Let me speak. You promised to let me speak. All right, no, I am not
a transgendered person. You're right about that. But I'm a woman.
And do you know a woman's choices these days as a writer? I'll
tell you, you've got two choices, you've got—well you can write
experimental, feminist, thought-provoking novels about whores
or bad girls that no one will read, or you can write touching,
romantic-garbage crap about women who have been molested
coming to terms with themselves and looking inside themselves and
finding their true nature, going on a journey which ends with love
and healing and self-acceptance. Oprah Winfrey crap. You know
what? I spit on that. I spit on that garbage. I am a woman, and I am
a writer, but why the fuck can't I write a real, dark novel about real
people about anything, about sex, about HIV, about promiscuity. Do
you know what I was before I started writing? I was a rock musician;
you say you're a rock musician so you know something about what
that's like, well I was an actual rock star, not a big one, but in New
York City we played at CBGB and I fucked and I played and I was
a groupie and I had groupies and I did the drugs and I LIVED, but
I can't write about that. I can't write about THE REALITY of that. I
would have to write a tell-all gossip thing or I would have to write
about a woman who got redeemed. Redeemed by love. Well, you
want to know the truth? Love doesn't redeem you. You've got to
redeem yourself, buster, and the only one who loves you is you, and
you know what, this is not my main thesis, which I will get back
to in a second, trust me, but I will say this, I know it endangers my

case with you but I've got nothing to lose, buster, I've got nothing to lose at this point, let me just say that if you are in such a sorry state that the only way you can respect yourself is if you see yourself reflected in a goddamn novel, if you expect a novel to redeem you, well let me tell you something, this is not Oprah, honey, you have to REDEEM YOURSELF. Because the world does not reflect back the true you, it does not reward you. If anything the world PUNISHES excellence. I was an EXCELLENT rock musician and I was punished. I was PUNISHED because a woman is not a rock musician and not a sexual outlaw, she is either a slut or she finds fucking God, I don't know, listen to me, listen, I feel for you, Jesus Christ what I go through is nothing. I'm just a woman, I'm just a fucking woman and what you tell me about Izzy—Jesus CHRIST, Izzy—who can only go out at night, what does that mean, what would it mean to live like that? I don't know, I can only imagine, but that's what I have done here, I have imagined. I have imagined something. And it was desperate and I was at the end of my rope because I've got something called an excess of personality, I've got it and it's not a diagnosed condition but it's me, and those of us with an excess of personality, we have to create SOMETHING or we will go crazy. It's not a choice, it's not something we consider, it's not politically correct, and let me tell you something, we create what we have to, and we create men, women, queers, transsexuals, dogs, we put ourselves into the heads of dogs sometimes we writers, why? Why? Because we can and because we must. If I followed what you said, which is saying, "Hey, you're not a transsexual, you don't have a right to write about them," where would we be? We would be without Shakespeare, we would be without every goddamn writer that ever lived. No, the answer is no, I am not you, I am not transgendered, I don't know about your experience. I wrote my experience, and I marketed it in the only way I knew it would be read and accepted and understood, I wrote it as what is trendy now—I know you wouldn't want me to say this, but what is trendy? Transgendered, being transgendered and being HIV-positive is just something that people are interested in reading about and I admit it, I'm a writer and I wanted to be read, is that a crime? I wanted to be read. And the most I think you can say, because you've lived what I've fictionalized, you've lived it—is that I've got it wrong and if that's what you want to say, I accept it, I really do, and I apologize, but let me tell you, if you go out there and say what you feel you have to say, all right, okay, go ahead, SAY IT. REVEAL ALL. I don't mind, I do mind, but I'll just tell them the truth, my truth. Because what I did ultimately was just try and get by. I gotta be me, too, you know? *(She sings a little.)* I gotta be ME. And ultimately, okay—I don't know if it's right to play these victim games and wonder who suffered more, we both suffered. And we're both… suffering now. So… since there's so much suffering in the world, wouldn't it be nice if we could just… be friends? Huh? Fuck, sure, huh, yeah. When it comes down to it. I just want to be your friend. *(Pause. She sits back on the desk, looks at JT.)* So what do you say?

YELLOW

TARA BEAGAN
DREARY AND IZZY

A proud half-breed of Ntlaka'pamux and Irish Canadian heritage, Tara Beagan was the 2011 playwright-in-residence at the National Arts Centre. Tara's plays include *Thy Neighbour's Wife* (three Dora nominations including an award for Outstanding New Play); *Dreary and Izzy*; *Here, Boy!*; *Miss Julie: Sheh'mah* (five Dora nominations); *Quilchena*; *Foundlings*; *BLUEBEARD'S WI7E*; *TransCanada*; *Anatomy of an Indian*; *The Mill: The Woods*; and *free as injuns*, inspired by Eugene O'Neill's *Desire Under the Elms* and "the Canadian Experience."

Nineteen seventy-five, Lethbridge, Alberta. When the Monoghan sisters lose their parents in a car accident, Deirdre becomes the sole caregiver to her older sister, Isabelle. Adopted as an infant from the neighbouring Blood Indian Reserve, Isabelle is loving, joyous, and severely affected by fetal alcohol syndrome in a time before this disorder had a name. Just as Deirdre is poised to enter university and begin exploring for the first time her own future and independence, she must choose how much of her own life she will sacrifice for the love of Isabelle.

Premiered at the Weesageechak Begins to Dance XVII Festival for Native Earth Performance Arts at Buddies in Bad Times Theatre, Toronto, in October 2004.

• • •

A bare light up on ISABELLE, *a First Nations woman in her late twenties, simple hairstyle, black clothing.*

ISABELLE

Sometimes, somehow... this voice gets through. The one you hear right now. Level. Sensible. Able. It's not here all the time— I don't even live here. And yet she never doubts who I am—always knows she's heard from me before. Each time I slip into her head, she knows that I belong with her somehow. I try to find a way to fill the space where I should be. Gently. I begin. Sometimes it is hardly a whisper. Barely noticeable. Like a soft hello—she catches a hint of it, she has to still herself to make it out. This voice. Only when she rocks herself, all alone and quiet, does she hear the steady sound... of a smart girl. I would make her strong. Wise. And whole. The woman she could have been. I seep in through the cracks, insisting to be heard— Loud. Clear. Angry. So keen, so sharp that she feels pain and her body is taken. And she is lost—for a minute, five minutes, an hour—her whole body clutches, shouts, and folds in on itself, suffering under the effort of trying to connect the Isabelle who exists with the Isabelle who cannot be. We fight each other, ourselves, this damaged brain, and I am newly broken, freshly wounded, to discover that I cannot come forward in a body that has seized. I can only exist when this body is well. She can't hear me without the pain of knowing what has been lost, taken... and so I stop. I leave her. I still myself until I am invisible again. And she goes back... out there, and I am deeper yet, inside. And she becomes herself again. The Isabelle you know.

We hear DEIRDRE's *voice coming from the darkness, overlapping with* ISABELLE's *voice and in the background.*

She is returned to the existing world.

• • •

DEIRDRE

And she did for a while. Feel better. We found our space together in this house. Just the two of us. Then she started to feel tired all the time and sick in the mornings. The doctor said she was due in April. For a little while I try to believe that I can look after Isabelle and the baby. But I keep thinking how much it was just to look after Izzy. And look how that went.

She gets to take some of her things with her. The Michener Centre has strict policies that are meant to keep other residents from feeling unfavoured. The other things go to the Salvation Army.

ISABELLE *enters, in a near catatonic state, wearing a thick, blue terry-cloth robe.* DEIRDRE *does not acknowledge her.*

Her room is small. She shares it with a girl who is barely there. Skin and bones and not a word. Isabelle's not there a month and I move up to Red Deer—even though they don't let family visit for the first year. I get hired with the cleaning staff at the Michener

Centre—graveyard shift. Nobody knows she's my sister. I visit her while she sleeps. Tell her about the things that have happened— real and made up. Bedtime stories. One story every night. I tell her where her things went. Her favourite things they wouldn't let her keep—the white dresser, her baby dolls, her Barbie car—and I try to think of a good place where they've ended up. I tell her the story of how her jewellery box was given to this little six-year-old Cree girl in Hobbema on her birthday. She has no jewellery, but she fills the box with the prettiest rocks she can find in the neighbour's driveway—she shines them up with her mom's clear nail polish, locked in the bathroom and hunched over her work, making sure she doesn't spill any.

I tell her about the night her son was born—pulled from her belly while she slept. I don't tell her how I nearly screamed out loud when I saw his red curly hair, how I had to stop myself from running to find a phone. Call information for "Seven Horses." The next night I come in for my shift and the baby is gone—adopted by a rich couple in Indiana.

> ISABELLE *sits beside* DEIRDRE, *not seeing her.* DEIRDRE *now speaks to* IZZY. *During the following,* ISABELLE's *arms rest at her side, allowing her robe to fall open, revealing a pale blue hospital gown soaked through with breast milk.*

One night while I'm visiting, a nurse comes in, so I pretend to empty the empty garbage can. She doesn't even look my way as she sits you up and pulls down your covers. You're still the same—you don't wake up even if you're seated upright and spoken to. The nurse doesn't ask me to leave. She lifts your nightgown to check your stitches and change your dressings, and so I sweep the floor, needing to know how you're doing. The nurse reaches for the garbage can, so I hold it up. I see the milk-soaked cotton gauze land in the tin basket with a dull wet thud. The nurse tucks fresh pads inside your gown, to absorb the milk your breasts will not stop making. Milk for a son you will never hold. She finally leaves and I tuck you in. Tight.

Born, raised, and based in Vancouver, Filipino-Canadian author C. E. Gatchalian writes drama, poetry, fiction, and non-fiction. He is currently the artistic director of the frank theatre company. His plays, which include *Broken*, *Crossing*, *Claire*, and *Motifs & Repetitions*, have appeared on stages nationally and internationally, as well as on radio and television. Recent work includes his play for young audiences, *People Like Vince*, which was commissioned by Green Thumb Theatre and toured BC, Saskatchewan, and Ontario, and his latest play, *Falling in Time*, which premiered in Vancouver in November 2011, was published by Scirocco Drama, a division of J. Gordon Shillingford Publishing in 2012, and was a finalist for the Lambda Literary Award. He is the winner of the 2013 Dayne Ogilvie Prize, awarded annually by The Writers' Trust of Canada.

Falling in Time centres on the miraculously intertwining lives of four characters. A meditation on war, masculinity, sexuality, personal boundaries, and love, *Falling in Time* asks the question, how do we let go?

Steve, sixty-five, an American living in Vancouver, has been diagnosed with AIDS. In denial, he continues his hard-living ways. While in the gym one day he encounters Chang Hyun, and meeting the young Korean triggers memories of one of the defining events of his life: the Korean War. He is rugged and handsome, and looks younger than his age.

Premiered at Performance Works in Vancouver in November 2012, produced by the frank theatre company (then Screaming Weenie Productions) in association with the Meta.for Theatre and the Vancouver Playhouse.

● ● ●

Sound effects: Bar. People talking and laughing, glasses clinking, etc.

STEVE

I tell ya… *(Lights up on* STEVE *in a bar, on a stool, drink in hand, inebriated, talking to some unseen other.)* The Canucks have gotta fucking brush up on their defence. Did you see that game against the Rangers? Fucking incompetence. 3–2, five minutes left in the third. A fucking one-goal lead they had and the Rangers quiet as pansies. Then some fifth-line teenybopper from a farm team ends up tying it. How in hell on God's green earth did that fucking happen? I'll tell you how: they fucking fell asleep. They may as well have emptied the ice and the net coz the path was fucking clear for them to score that goal. Jesus, they fell asleep. But they're playing for a sleepy-ass city—how can they *not* fall asleep? Even my hometown in Indiana had more get-up than this lotus-roost. You know what happens when people fall asleep, buddy boy? They die. They fucking die. I, for one, never sleep. Okay, I nod off a coupla hours

or so but I don't sleep the way others do, and you know why? Coz
sleep's for sissies. It's—

*Lights snap out, one-count. Lights up. Again he is talking to some
unseen other.*

Kimchi, you know what kimchi is, don't you? You don't? What, you
just crawl out of the backwoods? You've never heard of kimchi?
Where you from? Surrey? Kimchi, *Christ*, it's only the best food
ever created. It gets you revved up, it gets you all horny—I fucked
like a rabbit when I was back in Korea. A lot of Korean bitches had
a fill of this here *(points to his crotch)* and are happier women for it.
You think in a million years they'd get what I gave them from *their*
men? They're a bit... under-blessed, to put it, as they say, delicately.
But kimchi, *fuck*, it made a warrior out of me. I'd sneak as much as
I could into the barracks and I'd eat it every morning, I'd get this
fucking rush and my day'd be all set. I got into amazing shape—my
biceps were hard as melons *(flexes his biceps)*—still got them, by
the way, not bad for a pensioner. But more important I was a great
soldier, so great that after the war I decided to keep doin' it, coz it
was my vocation, my calling, like some are called to the priesthood.
Did I tell ya that during the war I got by on a measly two hours of
sleep every day? When everyone else was asleep I was busy doing
push-ups. Coz you know what happens when people sleep, don't ya?
They die, they fucking die.

*Lights snap out, one-count. Lights up. Again he is talking to some
unseen other.*

Boxers today—they got nothing on Marciano. Saw him fight his last fight. Live in Yankee Stadium, two years after Korea. Caught a hop there from Fort Riley. The most beautiful moment of my life. A fucking gladiator he was. Bullet-like passes, both hands, *both hands*. Then he'd work his way in and wham-BAM the uppercut, Moore's head snapping back like a petal off a daisy. Now he floored Rocky in the second but Rocky came storming back, he wasn't about to let his perfect record slip away. He knocked the sucker down five, count 'em, five times. *(throwing punches in the air)* Right, left, right right, DOWN. Left, right, right, left, DOWN, DOWN, DOWN, DOWN! *(He yelps with glee.)* 49 and 0. Perfection attained. Blood, vomit, and yellow-skinned commies. But at home, in that ring, there was God.

Lights snap out, one-count. Lights up. Again he is talking to some unseen other.

Jazz. You like jazz? What d'ya mean, you hate it? More like you don't understand it. You can't hate what you don't understand, now can you? There's no shame in admitting you're stupid. In fact more people should—the world would run a hell of a lot smoother if they did. If *you*, for example, would just admit *you're* stupid, you wouldn't be here arguing with me now and we'd both be having a nicer time. I heard 'em all, *live*... Charlie Parker, Miles Davis, John Coltrane, Lester Young. Saw Billie Holiday in a club in Cincy. A year from the grave and looking like a pile of bamboo sticks, long gloves to cover the needle marks, high as a fucking kite. But it didn't matter—she was singing, singing in that special way of hers, like she didn't fucking care, except you knew she cared too much. I swear if teardrops had a voice, they'd sound like Billie Holiday. The lifeline, I called it—that's what her voice was, this line from the soul that carried all of life's wears and tears. The last song she sang that night was "'Tain't Nobody's Business If I Do." Chin up, brow arched, it was like she was saying, "Ain't gonna change, ain't following no law but my own. Gonna keep going, ain't never giving up."

Lights snap out.

DIANA TSO
RED SNOW

Diana Tso is a performer/playwright/poet/storyteller who graduated from the University of Toronto with an Honours BA in English Literature and from L'École Internationale de Théâtre Jacques Lecoq, in Paris, France. She has worked with diverse theatres internationally for over 15 years. Her favorite theatre co-creations/performances include: *Dante's Inferno* and *Chekhov's Shorts,* both with Theatre Smith-Gilmour; as well as *and by the way, Miss...* with Urge/Theatre Direct, for which she shares the Dora Mavor Moore Award for Outstanding Ensemble Performance. Her *Monkey Queen, Journey to the East,* which premiered at the Toronto Storytelling Festival 2010, is a one-woman performance creation inspired by the Monkey King stories in Wu Cheng'en's sixteenth-century Chinese novel, *Journey to the West.* More information about Diana and her work is available at www.redsnowcollective.ca.

Red Snow is inspired by survivors of the 1937 Rape of Nanking. Isabel's recurring nightmare of her grandparents' favourite Chinese opera, *Peony Pavilion,* her grandfather's adamant silence regarding the war, and her recent discovery of one of his Chinese calligraphy poems written in blood drive her to China to find their silenced story and to find a way to help her family heal. There she meets Jason, a young Japanese man, whose ancestors were responsible for the holocaust of which her family is victim; their journeys collide as they both struggle to reconcile the past with the present.

When Isabel brings Jason home to meet her family, her grandfather, Gung Gung, vehemently demands the young man stay away from his granddaughter. Isabel and Jason's relationship opens a Pandora's box of family secrets that lead to this scene where Gung Gung relives the rape and murder of his wife, Popo, at the hands of Japanese soldiers during the Rape of Nanking.

The play premiered at Theatre Passe Muraille in January 2012, produced by Red Snow Collective, in association with Toronto ALPHA and Aluna Theatre, and was remounted at the Shanghai International Contemporary Theatre Festival in November 2012.

• • •

GUNG GUNG

飛揚塵土，越肩而過，落在我饑疲背影。
父母生離，兄妹死別，全部拆散。
身披鐵甲軍服的鬼魅，
揮下大刀如銀扇，
黃土飛揚，垂吊天涯。
千萬愁容，若隱若現，
雪花怒飛，捲起牡丹紅，隨風四散。

Fēiyáng chéntǔ, yuèjiān ér guò, làzài wǒ jīpí bèiyǐng.

Fùmǔ shēnglí, xiōngmèi sǐbié, quánbù chāisàn.

Shēnpī tiějiǎ jūnfú de guǐmèi,

Huīxià dàdāo rú yínshàn,

Huángtǔ fēiyáng, chuídiào tiānyá.

Qiānwàn chóuróng, ruòyǐn ruòxiàn,
Xuěhuā nùfēi, juǎnqǐ mǔdān hóng, suífēng sìsàn

English translation of the poem above:

lifting earth over my shadow
fathers, mothers torn away from brothers, sisters
phantoms in ironed uniform strike with curved silver fans
under a yellow smudge hanging in the sky
hundreds of thousands anguished faces
a fury of snow and red peonies

Hong Huang!... Hide under the table... *(half singing, half speaking)*
Life wraps its light around you... Life wraps its light around you...

Light falls on GUNG GUNG *as he relives the following.* GUNG
GUNG's *words are reflected in* POPO's *movements as she re-en-*
acts her rape and murder.

The doors burst open. They stuff my mouth with a rag soaked in
kerosene. They throw me into a chair and tie me to it, the weight of the
soldiers' hands pressing down on my shoulders, gripping my neck...
Hong Huang... she is with child...
They make me watch... one soldier... after the other...

POPO *screams in silence.*

Hong Huang!... They delivered our baby... on... a... bayonet...

POPO slowly pulls a red silk ribbon from her belly symbolizing the murder of her child being torn from her womb and the endless blood flowing from her belly.

They laugh... they dance... take pictures. They march out of our home... singing their national anthem...
POPO moves the red silk ribbon, like flames slowly rising, violently up above her head and to the sides.

One devil stays, takes the rag out of my mouth, lights a cigarette, sets the match on the rag... throws it onto her body...
Everything bursts into flames...
my wife... my child....

POPO exits slowly, pulling the red ribbon of blood with her to the afterlife.

Which little piece of ash is my wife?! Which speck of ash is my baby?! Where have they gone?

Silence.

PETER ANDERSON
THE BLUE HORSE

Playwright/actor Peter Anderson, well-known for his performance in *The Overcoat* and as a co-creator of *The #14*, lives in Vancouver where he has received six Jessie Richardson Theatre Awards. During his long association with the Caravan Farm Theatre, he has written over a dozen plays, including *Head Over Heels, Horseplay* (with Phil Savath), *The Coyotes, Bull by the Horns, The Ballad of Weedy Peetstraw,* and the mystery cycle trilogy *Creation, Nativity,* and *Passion.* Other plays include *Rattle in the Dash* and adaptations of *Don Quixote* (with Colin Heath) and *Lysistrata.*

Sooz, an alienated sixteen-year-old, finds herself at the center of a farcical chain of events when her journal musings take on a life of their own in this modern fairy tale/coming-of-age romance. Featuring a mysterious stranger in a powder-blue suit, a policeman who always cries, a one-hundred-year-old woman with one hundred horses, a backwoods conspiracy theorist, and a shape-shifting blue horse (who appears as a man in this monologue).

Premiered at the Caravan Farm Theatre in Armstrong, BC, on July 26, 2007.

• • •

The blue horse—in the shape of a man—enters, dripping wet, breathing heavily, carrying a body. He lays the body down, stops, stands still, staring at audience for a long time.

I feel their thighs squeezing, the sweat of their thighs forming patterns of salt like ancient lakes long gone and receded, a stain that remains, thighs pressing upon me moisture mingling with mine, winey smell of love-making, we're one and the wind, cool wind as we wind through the woods we're one seeking water, water we come from to which we return, the call of the river rising within, the trickle and trill, babble and bubble, blood bucking and rearing a galloping beat, sweat pouring freely, flesh become liquid, liquid then steam rising like fog, dew misting, condensing, droplets on leaves dripping in pools bleeding to soil feeding the forest, following the flow falling down over rocks, rivulets and rills, brooks, tributaries spilling spill spilling, into the stream, a river of dream eddying, swirling, flashing, and splashing, drowning sorrow, plunged under in wonder, the watery faces form and reform, ripples like wrinkles passing over expressions, weightless words washed away to the sea salt womb water mother umbilicus whoosh of the waves saltchuck slide and suck of the sand on the shore slipping and sliding all flows to the sea, back to the birth, the oneness, the wonder, the way of the watery world where no difference is, all memories mixed-up, mute, and marine, mariners of love, moments remembered the most, most moments of uppermost being alive and in love, living but then... Exiled again, yearning for closeness, connection, oh to be close to,

but always the fear, I am a monster, a story gone wrong, a nightmare of desire, never fulfilled, never at peace, never content, neither
human nor horse, exiled and reviled, darkness, the cold, stars like
sharp spurs, distant lassoes of fire, some try to tame me, others to
blame me, shame me, lame me till she came to save me, her voice
called from the river, a cauldron of dreams culled from the river, O
to be human not mute in my hoarseness not hoarse in my muteness
awaken and shaken out of the dream onto dry land upright with a
voice to dance on two feet to sing, speak, be spoke to, tell jokes to,
be loved and be laughing, not haunted nor hunted, not other, alone,
but to be one with her stepping lightly light lightly to form words
on the tongue taste thought give mouth to the heart in the flesh and
blood world of the dreamer who dreaming dreamed me into being.

Nina Arsenault is a Toronto-based trans-discipline artist and personality. Her life and her work blur traditional lines between art and artist, character and actor, performance and reality. Working in live performance, photography, video, writing, and other media, she has continued to document and explore her continuing psychic and physical transformations. The focus of past transformations have been the body, gender, beauty, celebrity, and faerie.

The Silicone Diaries is seven real-life stories from transsexual Nina Arsenault, who has undergone sixty cosmetic alterations, a journey that spanned eight years and took a lifetime of preparation. Each story explores the continuing joy and tumult written on, through, and throughout her body as she struggles with the contradictions that surround the pursuit of inner and outer beauty.

Set in 2006, with most of the surgical refinements complete, Nina is at the height of her beauty in this scene.

Premiered at the Saint John Theatre Company in August 2008 as part of their Out On the Edge Festival.

PLAYWRIGHT'S NOTE

The reality of beautifying surgical procedures is that when they are fresh their glamour can be dazzling. Add to this eyeliner, the accoutrements of glamour like false lashes and good lighting, and the effect can be, for better or worse, almost inhuman. The augmentations to the flesh do not age naturally and they *transmogrify* very quickly. Far more rapidly than I was prepared for. Gravity weighs upon the heavy silicone. Pulled skin like an elastic band (if you'll excuse the grotesque example) longs to return to its untethered tension, but it can no longer do so naturally. The trajectory of the flesh has been realigned forever—on the surface and beneath. We are not accustomed to seeing how a worn surgical face could once have been beautiful. It is not like looking at the face of an alluring mature woman and seeing how she must once have been a stunning young beauty. The changes are unnatural and the ways they wane are unfamiliar. In many ways, the surgically altered person is the last one to discover this cruel aspect of time on our face. In this, and in thinking that Glamour is a worthy pursuit, I have played the willing Fool. Still, I am unashamed for these tragical life lessons. They do not alter the present truths of my past stories.

—Nina Arsenault, November 2013

ME 'N' TOMMY LEE

NINA

One night, before heading to Ultra Supper Club, I pop an Ativan. Ativan's a mild tranquilizer, less than a Valium. It takes away my anxiety, but also some inhibitions wash away too. I give in to a primal urge to tease my hair up with a magnificence usually reserved for porn stars and Vegas showgirls. I paint my eyeliner so intricately.

What a gorgeous pill.

As I glide into Ultra Supper Club, the restaurant manager, Neil, leads me by the hand, passing a line-up of over-the-top, skeleton-thin, silicone-enhanced women. Lots of extensions. Lots of rocker chicks.

Neil says, "Ugh! All wannabe star-fuckers. Here for the biggest-dicked rocker in the world."

He sweeps me to a seat on one side of the restaurant, directly facing, on the other side of the restaurant, what looks to me like former Mötley Crüe drummer and reality TV star, Tommy Lee. Tommy is seated behind a twinkling, translucent curtain. That curtain gives him a sparkling aura. Or maybe that's my drugs. Or maybe that's celebrity.

Neil pulls out my chair and compliments the shimmery grey slacks that I am wearing—they are skin-tight to my hips and ass—and the low-riding black latex tube top that hangs off the top of my new boob job, very swollen at the time. Neil says, "Darling, tonight, your ensemble could be a classed-up version of Pamela Anderson's wardrobe from the movie *Barb Wire*." Right then, I know that Tommy Lee is real, because that's the punchline of Neil's joke: Tommy Lee used to be married to Pam, and I take the reference to Ms. Anderson as a compliment. She is the ultimate silicone sex symbol of all time, and I'd say she was the Marilyn Monroe of the '90s.

Neil offers me sparkling water.

High, I reply, "Sparkling wine would be lovely. Thank you very much."

The Ativan mingles with the champagne. All of a sudden, I am happy. In fact, I am radiating a child-like, innocent joy and confidence that only a careful combination of dissociative drugs can give you. I know that I've created quite a stir, that all eyes in the restaurant are locking onto me, but I have Ativan-reinforced self-esteem. Nothing gets through that. Because I'm not wrapped up in my own self-consciousness, I can see, upon closer inspection, that most of the women here purposefully trying to catch Tommy's attention are poorly painted and half-dressed, with all the class of off-duty Hooters waitresses. I usually don't let myself judge people like that, but the Ativan has really lowered my inhibitions. I drink in their stares with a smile, and chase them down with another glass of champagne.

I'm radiant. My inner calmness is a light that is filling a room full of women posing nervously, and I'm visualizing on my interior screen, in my mind's eye, that Tommy Lee can't take his eyes off me. Even though I never look over at him. Not even once. Believing it so easily. The way a child believes. It's already happened, the way I am seeing it.

A man comes to the table, saying he's Tommy's associate, and tells me that the rock star wants to meet.

I say, "I'm in the middle of dinner," referring to untouched salmon and grilled vegetables, having a little bit more champagne. I am not a disposable, fart-catching bimbo for a rock star who's claimed to have had slept with "a *lot* more than a thousand women." That's one of his Wikipedia quotes! He's slept with "a *lot* more than a thousand women." "*Lot*" is in italics.

But after his man leaves, I think, Tommy Lee has an employee pick up his chicks. It's fabulous. He never has to face rejection.

The employee didn't even know I'm a transsexual. Maybe just having enough confidence to feel that I belong, drug-induced or not, makes me belong. I'm thinking about the power of that, the entire time visualizing on the interior screen in my mind's eye that my rejection of Tommy Lee has made me all the more attractive to him. Before I know it, his representative is at my table again, saying, "No, no, no, no, no, no, no. Tommy *really* wants to meet you. He thinks that you are fabulous."

I think, Nina, you cannot cut yourself off from everything life has to offer just because you're afraid people will reject you for being a transsexual. Besides, it's a huge ego boost to be hand-picked out of a pack of posing, real women. Many of whom are very beautiful, upon second glance, despite what I consider very incorrect, low-class, trashy fashion. But I get it. Straight men often find low-class women very enticing for a night.

I stand.

The women scoff at me. It's like I can see their thoughts on their faces.

"Why her?"

"That fake plastic bitch?"

"That's a man!"

I shade these Tommy Lee-rejects with a downwards cast of my extra long lashes at the 45-degree angle, which everyone knows is the shadiest angle possible, and by flipping my head to the side, knowing that the four bags of fake 28-inch-long hair extensions look positively pornographic as they cascade through the air to bounce off my glowing, tanning-cream-bronzed shoulder. I see the moment as if I am outside myself. As if I am watching a slow-motion snippet from a movie. I'm the star of the movie now.

A powerful feeling of fierceness is coursing through me as I walk towards a man who was married to one of the most revered sex symbols of all time. On the way over, I dare to compare myself to *the* Ms. Pamela Anderson. Kohl-ringed eyes, teased hair, enormous breast implants, and a trademark teeth-together-lips-apart lusty expression of come-hither-ness. She is a caricature of a woman. Tonight I am a caricature of her. An imitation of an imitation of an idea of a woman. An image which has never existed in nature, but singled out as the shining beauty in the room.

I can't believe this is happening to me. I'm the person who was always told she would never be accepted as a woman.

I'm slipping behind the glimmering, semi-opaque drapes that divide the common dining area from the celebrity VIP section where Tommy Lee and his entourage are seated. I think, "I'm fierce enough to do it. I can make Tommy Lee fall for me." I will drop a powerful feeling of belonging deep inside of me, and he will see how truly fabulous I really am.

I approach boldly. I crouch low, next to Tommy's chair, and shake his hand, a little trick I learned at the tranny strip club where I work. It combines the flattering angle of looking upwards into the man's face with the mental suggestion that you could at any moment give him a blow job, right there in front of everybody. I like to offset the sleaze factor of this position by smiling sweetly, and by looking up into the scintillating light of an overhead, dangling chandelier, knowing that it will make my makeup sparkle at just the right angle.

Yes, I think all these thoughts around a man I want to seduce.

Tommy says, "Whhoooooaaaaa. You are extraordinarily beautiful."

Ex-tra-or-din-ar-i-ly. It's a seven-syllable word. My beauty inspires Tommy Lee to use a seven-syllable word.

He looks better in person than on TV. I don't want to think he's Botoxing. I'm seeing everything through the haze of a champagne-Ativan cocktail. He looks just like one of my ex-boyfriends. We're making a bit of small talk. Fuck, we're getting along so well. My confidence amplifies my sex appeal by a factor of ten.

Now, Tommy is looking at me with a look in his eye that says, "Wait a minute. Is she…? Is that…? Is…?"

I drop in a powerful feeling of complete and total belonging and maintain eye contact. It smoothes the whole moment over.

He asks me if I want to do drinks.

I say, "Yeah, let's do shots of tequila."

They're at the table like *that* 'cause when you're Tommy Lee that's how fast your tequila gets to the table.

I throw mine back.

Tommy chokes on his: "Ghack!"

He says he's been drinking since 7 a.m., about fifteen hours ago now. I'm a little bit disappointed that a guy who has apparently snorted his own bandmate's piss can't throw back a shot of Cuervo. I'm also disappointed to see him eating something that looks like a deconstructed serving of pâté, decorated with a delicate array of Asian greenery. Hardly what I consider rock star food.

I guess a lot of us have a public image out there that does not encapsulate the complexity of who we really are. But I still say, "You're a fucking pussy!"

Tommy says, "Someone get this girl a chair."

Members of his entourage are looking around the VIP section for a chair.

I am not going to act star-struck. I will portray a ballsy, glamour-puss-type of chick, the kind of chick who talks fast and parties hard: exactly the kind of fantasy of a woman I imagine Tommy Lee could fall for. I will make her so real.

When an extra chair can't be found, Tommy invites me to share his. There's not enough room on that chair for Tommy and for my hips and ass.

I can't believe how well things are going between us. It's hard to remember that your actions have consequences when you're this excited, when you're drinking, when you're popping dissociative pills... and I do something I never do.

I ease myself onto the unwitting lap—I don't know what he knew— of Tommy Lee. On the surface I'm totally cool because of the Ativan. Inside, inside, inside... I'm freaking out.

He asks me what I do for a living.

"I'm an exotic dancer." I don't mention that it's a strip club for trannies.

He wraps his arms around me in a tight embrace. He gives me a double "thumbs up" and goes, "Aaaaaaaaiiiiiieeeeeeeee!"

He pulls me into him, and he pushes up into me. The base of Tommy's dick. There's so much dick down there. I can feel it. I can feel all that dick. I'm drunk on male attention when I'm sitting on that much dick.

Time seems to stop.

On the interior screen, in my mind's eye, a life with me and Tommy Lee is flashing by. First we go back to his hotel room and we fuck like animals all night long, recording everything on his camcorder. The footage leaks to online celebrity blog sites like perezhilton.com and TMZ.com. Two days later, on *Entertainment Tonight*, Mary Hart's eyes are filling with tears of joy as Tommy defends the film and declares, "I love her." They have paparazzi night-vision video footage of Tommy and me, in and out of LA nightclubs. Pamela Anderson is on his one arm. I'm on the other. The soundtrack is Tommy's old hit "Girls, Girls, Girls." No one thinks it's ironic. When they slow the footage down, you can see right into my eyes. You can see what I'm thinking. I'm thinking, "I love you, Tommy. Because you love me. I love what that must mean about my beauty."

It's getting harder to believe in this fantasy.

Back at Ultra Supper Club, I can see a member of Tommy's entourage mouthing the words, "That's a guy! That's a fucking guy!" The guy beside him is going, "How did we let this happen? How did this happen?" Each man whispers to the next. The news is travelling around the table. A countdown is ticking in my head. Ten, nine, eight, seven seconds until he finds out I have a dick, six, five, four. As each second goes by I shrink a little bit. Three, two, one.

When the news is whispered into Tommy's ear, he looks every part of me up and down. Feet, knees, hips, waist, tits, shoulders, Adam's apple, hair, and he stares directly into my face for what feels like an eternity. I don't know what to do, so I do this. *(gesturing a flower blossoming from her face with her hands)* A light-hearted gesture that I am hoping will suggest, in the softest possible way, "Surprise."

Tommy goes, "Woooaaaaaaaaaaaaah! You really *are* beautiful…"

I don't know if the subtext at the end of his sentence is "…for a man" or if he just likes the way I worked the whole encounter.

That brings me completely back together on his lap. I don't want to be made to feel less beautiful because I was born into a male body, or because I have fake parts. Everything that attracted you to me in the first place, Tommy Lee—synthetic hair, makeup, silicone, attitude, radiance—I don't have to be born a biological woman to have these things, and I want you to get that it is these things that give you the physiological feeling of a hard-on.

Maybe he gets it, because Tommy does this *(shaking head, shaking head again, shaking head a third time, shoulders dropping, breath dropping, then double thumbs up, smiling)* and says, "I need a cigarette."

Then, he slips out from under me, and he's out of the VIP section.

I steal one more glass of champagne off his table before that sea of jealous bitches can come for me, and I escape Ultra.

Gein Wong is a playwright, poet, and composer whose works have been performed in North America, the United Kingdom, the Caribbean, and East Asia. She appears on the *Dig Your Roots* Canadian Spoken Word CD and is a New York Kundiman Poetry Fellow. She was shortlisted for the 2010 K.M. Hunter Theatre Award and is currently developing *Hiding Words (for you), (we once gave) Shelter, Tent City,* and *Drawn.* Other playwriting credits include *Salt, Fish Girl 1,* and *How We (For)got Here* (co-writer). She is published in *Strike the Wok* and *ToK2: Writing the New Toronto.* She is Artistic Director of Asian Arts Freedom School and Eventual Ashes. Visit www.geinwong.com for more information.

Hiding Words delves into *nushu,* a secret language that Chinese women created when they were not allowed to read or write. Set in China on the eve of its biggest nineteenth-century rebellion, as well as a present-day Canada with heightened national security, this play examines the relationship between two women who are connected with each other through space and time.

Grace Lee has been held in a detention centre under suspicion of espionage activity. She is tired, confused, and hungry when an old red cloth seemingly appears out of nowhere. The cloth has strange poetic writing stitched into it.

Premiered in a workshop reading at Factory Studio Theatre, Toronto, in January 2010, presented by Eventual Ashes with dramaturgy by Jean Yoon.

• • •

GRACE LEE
What does this one say? I... mmm... I search... no, that's not right... I... I grasp... No no... I learned, yes, yes it's I learned...

I learned to write
for you.
Who are so far away,
ten thousand footsteps
would not bring us,
close,
enough.

I learned to write for you.
With needle and thread.
Stitched to be hidden,
in cloth and decorations.
Can you read these words?
Will you understand?

Ten thousand hopes I've had.
Each one woven
with threads of disappointment,

in frustration.
A girl lost in Guangzhou.
Who dreams of a place where
people listen,
who dreams
of choices
made myself.
Who dreams.

And now I can only think of you.
Of reaching out and touching your hand.
Of dancing
freely in the streets,
with you
sharing mango and taro,
with you.
Looking into your eyes
and knowing it's the right time
to laugh.

So I sew this with needle and thread.
Keep it with me in the bed where I sleep.
With hopes that you can decipher.
Words within fabric.
Songs that sound like secrets.
My sworn sister,
I'm hiding this,
for you…..

Thomas Morgan Jones is a Toronto-based director, playwright, dramaturg, instructor, and movement coach. His productions have received seven Dora Mavor Moore Awards and three further nominations. He received the 2011 Dora Mavor Moore Award at the Tyrone Guthrie Awards (Stratford Festival), and has been nominated for the Pauline McGibbon Award and the John Hirsch Director's Award (in both 2008 and 2011). He has collaborated with companies including Theatre Direct, the Stratford Festival, Theatre Passe Muraille, Cahoots Theatre Company, Theatre Rusticle, Buddies in Bad Times Theatre, Carousel Players, Theatre Jones Roy, the CULTCH, the Charlottetown Festival, Cia Enviezada (Brazil), and many others. He holds a B.A. from the University of Guelph, an M.A. from the University of Toronto, and recently trained with SITI Company in NYC, Madrid, and Paris. He is currently playwright-in-residence with Shakespeare in Action, an artist educator in residence with Young People's Theatre, and associate artist with Theatre Direct.

Susan has been diagnosed with cancer. Throughout her treatment she comes to terms with her own fear as she navigates the deterioration and reinvention of her marriage to her husband, Samuel, and her responsibilities as a mother to her beloved daughter, Melody. Together, Susan and Samuel discover how the family will go on through Susan's strength and determination.

Susan worries that she will not be as good of a mother to her daughter as her own mother was to her.

Premiered in Vancouver in 2003, produced by the ad hoc group pomo dojo.

• • •

SUSAN

I'm here. What's it going to be tonight? A story. Right. I don't think we'll do one of the usual ones. I think I should tell you about… I have so many things to tell you about. I'll tell you a story about my mommy. A long time ago—long long long time ago—when she was a little girl. My mommy told me that her mother used to sing to her. Mommy got sung to all the time. That's right, just like you.

One day her daddy was called to war. The first one. My mommy said that when her daddy went off to war, she had begged him not to go. Not like you beg for more cookies, though, she really really begged. She said he smiled then, and she said that he had perfect teeth. Perfect. He kept trying to tell her not to worry, "Don't worry, my darling." That's what he would say. My darling. She's scared though, right? Scared like you get sometimes when I close the door all the way before you go to bed, even though you know that there's nothing in the room that can hurt you. The feeling that something's wrong, that you can't explain but it's there and you're not sure why but it is even though you can't explain it. She was scared. That's why she begged. So, her daddy bends down, smiling, perfect. He says to her, "Learn to sing." He says that if she learns to sing then she can sing him home from the war. He didn't know either… he didn't know what would happen in the war. So he tells her to sing and that he'll hear it, right? All the way over there he'll hear it and that's how he'll know how to come home. So he goes off and your great-grandmother started taking her to singing lessons. They suffered for the money too, but my mommy learned how to sing. She would sing to the sky every night. She would go out to her old paint-peeled porch every night and she would sing. She got to be the most beautiful singer. She became the woman she would become. She became my mother. *(beat)* He never came home. He never came home but she kept on singing every night on the paint-peeled porch, looking up at the perfect stars. Perfect.

She sang that same song, that same song that I sing to you that you'll sing to your children if you have them when you have them, that song that's our family's and our family's alone. You sing that song like I do like she did so that we know so that YOU know that no matter where we are that we're always with you. Whether you can see us or not.

My darling.

Now, go to sleep.

AHDRI ZHINA MANDIELA
WHO KNEW GRANNIE: A DUB ARIA

Founder and artistic director of the Toronto performing arts company b current, ahdri zhina mandiela is widely known as a director and
poet/performer. She has worked in the Canadian arts scene since the
late '70s—both independently and with companies like Black Theatre
Canada, Theatre Fountainhead, Canadian Stage Company, Company
of Sirens, Theatre In The Rough, and Black Theatre Workshop. She
is a multi-disciplined artist with works including dance choreogra-
phies, audio recordings, video shorts, and the seminal documentary
film, *on/black/stage/women*, which premiered on Canada's Bravo TV
network. mandiela is also the visionary and driving force behind
the highly buzzed rock.paper.sistahz festival, and the rAiz'n' the sun
Emerging Artist Training Program.

A stylized narrative that looks at dealing with changes in our lives
through the meeting of separated family for the burial of a dead
matriarch. The story revolves around several cousins who grew up
together: a blind teacher with a sixth-sense gift, a celebrity chef
who yearns to be accepted "back home," a musician/producer in
his darkest hours, a popular people's politician in her heyday, and
Grannie.

Vilma is a well-respected politician who is still "back home."
She is also still the one "in charge," just like when the cousins were
growing up.

Premiered at Factory Theatre, Toronto, in March 2010, produced by
Obsidian Theatre Company.

• • •

VILMA
she left without a toothbrush…
(with laughter) tears walled behind her eyes
one arm swinging slightly
while the other, weighted by a small neat/package
holding the only baggage she had ever stored
the previous sixteen years had been sweet
but now she wobbled inside the blur of each step
into the unknown/if only…
and then again, she did

so swallow hard every few steps
and welcome the sting with the soothe of the
one piece of ginger tucked beneath her tongue
for balance. at seventeen she was not prepared…
to leave. but she had to/leave.

an early morning rise was assured
as the nausea from that recurring cock's crow was her
new dawn.
feet to the floor, steady/steady

rise and shine for today/rise and shine… for today
is the first day of leaving this life

with her mother, her papa, her
from birth/redwooded quarters.
today was the first day of her 'i will never have this
life again'

and those indoors slippers will leave too...
patiently they lined the bottom of her boxed suitcase
decorated by hand
her sewing kit sitting next to them with ne'er a gripe

the threadbared nightgown off her back
found rebellion in its fold...
then the two pairs of bloomers, doubled from constant
shelf life
clung to near-tattered socks and one never-worn
stockings set...
and they decided to go too...

as did the three housedresses, two church set:
the book of songs stacked gently atop the older one
cased in pre-lunch brown paper, monogrammed for
posterity or
longevity or the uncertainty of chance; a sure-footed
belief
in that last rapturous dance
and the unmistakable branding of memories shored and
stored in past lives and this

and when the evening rustlers clucked and pecked and
brushed and settled
and poured onto their roosts, she knew this first night
would not be the hardest.
even with no brush for her teeth. her teeth with the
strained/scent
of mint and lime; those teeth unspoiled
from nearly seventeen years of cane and coco roots
and mango dinners
these teeth unspoilt from the daily duet of chewstick
and salt... were her only real keepsakes from that other
life/her younger/now past/old life

she knew this rumbling in her belly was not hunger
this new movement nearing the end of a second/trimester
this new movement/here/daring the beginning
this new movement wearing the swaddling of love
this new movement was hearing the hush of change
this new movement was in no rush

this new life, this case, this winsome morning she
grasped in her hands
knowing she with them must now travel into yesterdays
uttering few goodbyes, yelling no regrets
this life, this case, this alone-some morning
would send dust to the wind at her back
as she made an unfamiliar veer/away from home
a reluctant tilt onto that new leaf released in a fall from
grace.

MICHAEL RUBENFELD
MY FELLOW CREATURES

Michael Rubenfeld makes performance through a series of con-
texts including performing, writing, directing, and often producing.
His published plays with Playwrights Canada Press are *My Fellow
Creatures* and *Spain*. Michael has also made a series of works with
Sarah Garton Stanley, including *The Book of Judith* (co-creation), *The
Failure Show* (director), *mothermothermother...* (co-creation), and
they are currently creating a new work entitled *Oopsala*. Michael is
Artistic Producer of the SummerWorks Performance Festival (since
2008) and is a graduate of the National Theatre School of Canada's
acting program.

Two men, each serving time for the same crime, are forced to
question the nature of their desires when their pasts become their
present. Venturing into dark and explosive territory, *My Fellow
Creatures* is a raw, honest, and thoughtful portrayal of these men
and their virtues, confronting the reader with difficult questions
about love, consent, vengeance, and acceptance.

First produced by Absit Omen Theatre in association with Buddies
in Bad Times Theatre at Theatre Passe Muraille, Toronto, in May
2008.

• • •

ARTHUR

Did you use force?

Did you make him do anything he didn't want to?

Did he love you?

Did he tell you he loved you?

Beat.

Did he?

Did you love him?

Beat.

Did you tell him you loved him?

KELLY *nods his head.*

And did you believe that? When you looked at him. When you touched him. Did you believe, with all your heart, that you loved that child?

Beat.

I did.

I loved him.

He gave me love that I've never felt before. He wrote me letters. He was poetic. Ten years old. How many children are poetic?

They have so much love, Kelly. Did you not feel that? That trust? That unconditional love? That clarity.

To be trusted so fully. To give my love so fully.

To be sought after. To be touched. To be explored.

Such magical curiosity. Don't you see? We can't argue with the instincts of a child. We shouldn't.

Beat.

What we've done, we did for the right reasons. You have to believe that. It's all we have. Our integrity. Our love. You acted according to your honest feelings for another individual, and it's beautiful.

RAVI JAIN, KATRINA BUGAJ, TROELS HAGEN FINDSEN, AND NICOLAS BILLON
I'M SO CLOSE...

Founded in 2007, Why Not Theatre is a Toronto-based theatre company with an international scope. Under the artistic direction of Ravi Jain, Why Not has established a reputation as a company synonymous with inventive, experimental, cross-cultural collaborations resulting in shows featuring new Canadian writing and company-devised shows alongside revitalized interpretations of classics. Why Not is committed to exploring new forms of storytelling with a particular focus on the use of multimedia spectacles in a theatre deeply invested in the language of physical movement sharing the importance of the written and spoken text. Essential to our process are the collisions that arise from our different cultures, languages, and experiences. By combining various media with explosive physical energy we create stories that inspire alternative visions of existence. More information is available at www.theatrewhynot.org.

I'm So Close... is a heartbreaking love song, droned out by the hum of the technological landscape that is bringing us together and pushing us apart. We are living in a world where we are more connected than we have ever been. Technology allows us to communicate instantly across oceans, and develop relationships with those who we have never even met. As technological advances hit the market at an accelerating rate, one has to ask: how connected are we really? This monologue opens the play.

Premiered at the SummerWorks Theatre Festival, Toronto, in 2008.

• • •

MAN

Hi. Welcome. I want to thank you for choosing to spend your time with us this evening. I also want to take a minute to ask you to turn off your cellphones, if you haven't done so already.

He pulls out a cellphone and turns it off.

It always takes a second… It's funny to think of what we did before we had these things. Are you ready?

Seeing you all here makes me think about how we all got here. I mean, how did you get here?

Converses with the audience about how they got to the theatre, the distance they travelled, the time it took to get to the theatre from where they live.

You see, I find it so interesting to think about the time it takes to get from one place to another. And what really fascinates me, is the time it took for us to get *here,* to this moment in time. How *we* got *here.*

It all started with a big ferocious bang. And the result was billions of particles were sent floating in space, alone. And nobody likes to be alone. So these particles went in search of other particles. It's kinda like a high-school dance. You know, you're standing with your friends and then a slow song comes on and all of a sudden you look around and you are alone (or at least I was when I was in high school) because all your friends were dancing with partners. So you look desperately for someone to partner up with. And that is what these particles did, they partnered up into partnered particle pairs. And those partnered particle pairs partnered up with other partnered particle pairs and so on and so on until these particle pairs grew into larger and larger objects that eventually became planets. And on a certain number of these planets—at least one that we know of—life happened. So we are, in a sense, the children of promiscuous particles.

Now these planets are governed by a force called gravity. It's the force that keeps us in orbit, our feet on the floor and you in your seats. The thing is, that from the moment of that bang, the universe has been expanding, and though we don't feel it our planet is drifting further away from other planets and our galaxy is doing the same with other galaxies. Our fate is unknown. Either we will sail away into an abyss, or gravity will pull us all back together and smash us into bits, into a big crunch. Pretty bleak, no? But there is hope, because maybe, just maybe, that crunch will turn out to be another bang. Starting it all over again. Sending out billions of particles floating into outer space. Alone. And no one likes to be alone. So just maybe, those particles will go out in search of other particles, looking for connection, in this great cosmic dance.

DAVID S. CRAIG
NAPALM THE MAGNIFICENT: DANCING WITH THE DARK

David S. Craig has written twenty-nine professionally produced dramatic works including the international hit comedy *Having Hope at Home* (Blyth Festival), his adaptation of Carlo Goldoni's *The Fan* (Odyssey Theatre, Rideau Award for Best Adaptation), and *Danny, King of the Basement* (Roseneath Theatre, Dora Mavor Moore Award for Outstanding Production, German Children's Theatre Prize nomination), which has been seen by over half a million young people in North America alone. Other successful plays include *Smokescreen*, which has been translated into five languages.

These two monologues are taken from *Napalm the Magnificent: Dancing With the Dark* which is a play written for a three-foot bouffon. Bouffon is a style of theatre popularized by Philippe Gaulier. The character is not trying to make the audience like him. He loathes the audience for their stupidity, their cowardice, and their hypocrisy. However, to make his rants have more sting, he is charming, witty, and entertaining.

The play premiered at the Theatre Centre East, Toronto, in February 1995 in a co-production by Theatre Direct and Roseneath Theatre.

COFFEE

NAPALM

This is my coffee break. *(smells cup)* Mmmmmm. I love coffee.

This is a double shot cappa made from 100% high-altitude Columbian *mountain* beans. I've tried low-altitude beans but they just don't have the same flavour. Besides the coffee it's got organic milk, a touch of Torani almond syrup, which sinks to the bottom, and some Callebaut semi-sweet chocolate sprinkles which sits on the top. Hoo-yeah... Here goes. *(sips his coffee)* Mmmmmm! The first sip. Hot, frothy. Good. Very good. I feel pampered. I feel cared for. I feel loved. I deserve this.

If you could invent something that makes people feel this good for four bucks you'd make a fortune. Of course whatever you invent would have to cost you a lot less than four bucks. The coffee in this cup cost twenty-seven cents. The cup, sugar, cream, water, heating, and napkins cost another seventeen cents. That's a three and a half dollars profit. You sell five hundred cups a day and... bingo... over six hundred thousand profit. And that's without muffins. I don't eat muffins.

(sips) Mmmmmm. The second sip. I love the way the chocolatey froth sticks to my lips. I mention money because in our tribe we are not citizens, we are consumers. We vote with our credit cards and when you buy, someone wins and someone loses. Right now coffee is a big winner. Correction. Good coffee is a winner. And

where does good coffee come from? Columbia! Do you remember the cute ol' guy donkey? Juan! I loved that guy. He was so folksy. Well what's happening in Columbia is that anyone who has land is planting coffee. Well why wouldn't they? We want Columbian coffee and we'll pay in Yankee dollars, so let's tear out the banana trees, tear out the vegetables, and plant, plant, plant those arabica beans.

(sips coffee) This is my favourite part of the coffee experience. Now I can take nice big sips. There's one thing about coffee. It's not food. So when you replace food with coffee some people… have no food.

But that's not my problem. I just want a good cup of coffee. It makes me feel like a millionaire. What has my cup of coffee got to do with food in Columbia? Nothing. Where is Columbia? Nowhere. I mean do you really care about some coffee picker in Columbia? Of course not! Phew. For a second, I was beginning to feel "responsible." *(He sips.)* Pleasure.

He drops a nickel.

Five cents. That's how much a good Columbian coffee picker gets paid to pick a pound. The kids obviously get less.

He pours a pound of coffee on the nickel.

Thirteen million. That's the number of people who will die this year from malnutrition. Actually, that's not true.

He pours a bag of sand over the coffee.

Thirteen million is just the number of children under the age of six.

The last sip. Mmmmm. The coffee is cool now and I can taste the almond syrup. All gone, until next time. Did you notice the new kind of coffee cup they're using now? It's biodegradable. I think that's being really conscientious. Don't you?

He crushes the cup.

NICE PEOPLE

The speech begins sweetly.

NAPALM

You're good people. You're fine people. You're people who make your beds, and floss your teeth, and wash your hands when you wipe your bums. You're people who tell the truth and buckle up and hand in your work. You're people who co-operate with the police. Wow.

You're people who know the rules and play "the game" because you know "the game" was created by men and women of vision and wisdom. Elders of the tribe who love you, the way I do.

You're people who are living through huge economic and social changes. Changes that are ripping apart countries and families and opening doughnut stores on every corner.

You're people who say yes! Yes to life and friends, and fast and loud, and laughing, laughing so hard it hurts and you can't stop and then you pee your pants and laugh some more.

But you're also people who say "no." No to sexual stereotyping, racial discrimination, and the use of handguns for any reason... unless it's absolutely necessary... like in a business transaction, or for revenge purposes, but otherwise NO! And no to cigarettes, and drugs, and alcohol, and unprotected sex, and YES! Yes to environmental protection, yes to universal daycare, and yes, yes, yes to someone like me.

You're good people. Billions would like to be you. Billions all over the world would trade their wood fires, their tin huts, their rags, their disease, their rancid food, their stinking water, their fear, their despair, their death to be you right now watching me! They'd think watching me was paradise. But guess what? They're not here. You are. You're sitting at the top of the heap. You're sitting in the sun at the top of the shit pile. *(enraged)* And you think you fucking deserve it!!!

(sweet again) Of course you deserve it. You're good people. You live in a good country. The United Nations says that Canada is the best place to live in the world. And Toronto is the best city in Canada. Which means you are the luckiest and best people in the world.

Of course, if you're on welfare or using food banks, and thousands of you are, it may be hard to enjoy how lucky you are. Hunger may interfere with the appreciation of your good fortune. But hey, even if you're broke you still got the basics. Basics. Like when you turn on the tap, tap water comes out. Everyone in Canada has got that. Except our First Nations people… but I think that's part of their culture. Going down to the river, cutting a hole in the ice, dragging it back up to their huts in buckets. They like doing that kinda thing. It's outdoorsy. But for the rest of us, running water is basic. And flush toilets. Basic. You push a little chrome lever and all the stuff disappears. Where does it go? Who knows? Who cares? It's a miracle but everyone's got one. And a roof over your head. Everyone's got that. Except homeless people but that's just a personal choice. And a television, and a PVR—well c'mon, everyone's got a PVR. A PVR is basic. And thirteen years of free education, and subsidized university, and a job. Well I mean what was all this education for if you can't get a job? A job is basic. And then a car. I didn't say a new car. Just a basic car with a basic sound system and basic GPS with four-wheel drive. And a free, national, health-care system. That's really, really basic. Unless the government takes it away, in which case it's not basic anymore. Things are basic until they aren't. That's one of the rules. But hey, I think acne-free skin is basic. And diamond nose rings and love and money and a Broadway show with dancing girls and a big orchestra starring me, Napalm the Magnificent. Well okay, that might not be basic but it would be nice. Nice is basic. Everyone deserves a little nice now and then. Well not everyone. Starving people don't deserve nice. You know the ones on TV? The ones shuffling through some fly-choked refugee camp? They don't deserve nice. They don't deserve anything. They deserve to die like dogs in a ditch!

Hey, I'm just joking. I'm not saying they deserve to die and you don't. I'm just saying that's the way things are. Aren't they?

DON HANNAH
WHILE WE'RE YOUNG

Don Hannah is a playwright and novelist who lives in Toronto and Lunenburg County, Nova Scotia. He wrote *While We're Young* when was the inaugural Lee Playwright-in-Residence at the University of Alberta. As a dramaturg, he has worked for PARC, the Playwrights Theatre Centre, and the Banff Playwrights Colony. *Shoreline*, a collection of his plays, is available through U of T Press. His novel, *Ragged Islands*, received the Thomas H. Raddall Atlantic Fiction Award. His most recent plays are *There is a Land of Pure Delight*, *The Woodcutter*, and *The Cave Painter*, which won the Carol Bolt Award.

While We're Young begins in the present and, in Act One, each scene moves a generation backwards (2007, early 1970s, late 1930s, WWI, 1890s, and 1870). The six first-act stories are linked thematically and examine situations related to being young—first love, pregnancy, disputes with parents, going to war, etc. In the second act, the scenes move forward (starting in the 1870s) and are connected by plot; as the act progresses, chronology breaks down as the six stories become one.

Jamie is in his early twenties, from Moncton, New Brunswick, and has just arrived at the Front with his cousin Mac. Mac is asleep and Jamie is talking to Paul, who is also from Moncton and who Jamie has just met (Paul and Mac were childhood friends). It is winter, 1917.

Premiered at the Timms Centre for the Arts, Edmonton, in February
2008.

• • •

*January, Flanders, late afternoon, a trench. JAMIE talks to PAUL.
Nearby, JAMIE's cousin MAC is sleeping. Snow is falling.*

JAMIE

At the train station, last time I saw Sarah, he stood in front of us,
his back to us. My folks were there, too, but this was later 'cause my
father had to take my mother away. Crying so bad, and there was
always something with her and Sarah, she… My father took her
home. Then it was Mac there with the two of us, so he said, "Make
pretend I'm not here," and turned around. We were against the
station wall and he stood there in front of us, to give us some privacy.
I kissed her. I go back over it time and again. How long were we
there? Maybe a minute or two? But I can stretch it out forever. I can
go over it, each second, over and over. *(beat)* The baby there between
us, not yet a baby, not born, but there, with us. Mac's back was so
close, just— *(with his fingers indicates a couple of inches)* and the
stone wall, we were in a space between them. She was so close to me.
Closer than we had ever been together out in public like that. You
know, the way your mother or father is close and big when you're
small and they lift you up? And we were kissing and whispering at
the same time. When I reached inside her coat, and she took my
hand, and guided it. She had told me that she was so warm with
the baby that her clothes made her irritable sometimes—I realized

that beneath her coat—there was nothing beneath her blouse. I felt her, felt her skin, so tight where she had been so soft before, like a drum, you know, and there, beneath her skin, inside of her, the baby moving— I can't begin to tell you what it was like. The station and Mac all disappear and it's almost like we were in the bedroom on Mountain Road and—I'd been in Valcartier at camp, I hadn't seen her so big and—I wanted to be alone someplace with her, to press myself close. Put my ear against her and listen. Mac's shielding us so that we could kiss, I imagine he thought, but we were all caught up in what was happening inside her. It was so, so— I don't know how to talk about it, Paul. I don't know what to say or— For there's something unnatural about it. I know that sounds foolish but there it is. About having another thing grow inside of her. Unnatural is wrong, I mean, not real, somehow. Like a magic story. And I thought, "I'm not a kid anymore," and I thought about how hard it would be for her with me away from her for a few months. If only that moment could be stretched and stretched, long enough for the baby to be born and be held and... And she is now. Helen. If it was a girl we decided to call her Helen.

KEITH BARKER
THE HOURS THAT REMAIN

Keith Barker is a Metis artist from northwestern Ontario. He graduated from the George Brown Theatre School, moving on to become Artistic Associate at Native Earth Performing Arts. *The Hours That Remain* is his first full-length play, which won him the 2013 SATAward for Achievement in Playwriting.

Denise has spent the last five years dedicated to uncovering the truth behind her sister Michelle's disappearance. Haunted by loose ends, she begins seeing visions of Michelle, who gradually guides her in the right direction. As Denise's marriage and sanity crumble around her, she remains committed to unearthing an unfathomable truth, and coming to terms with a painfully crucial realization—one she has been desperately avoiding.

The Hours That Remain was first produced by New Harlem Productions and the Saskatchewan Native Theatre Company at Studio 914 in Saskatoon and the Aki Studio in the Daniels Spectrum Building in Toronto in October 2012.

• • •

MICHELLE

I'm sorry, but I've been mugged. Please help me.

I was putting some stuff in the back seat of my car when two guys jumped me.

You don't know where there's a pay phone, do you?

I used to roll my eyes at people when they told me to buy pepper spray for when I'm working late. All I could think about when it was happening was, "Dammit! I should have had something with me." I thought they were going to rape me, I really did— Look, I'm shaking.

Um… I, uh, I, uh, I walked up to my car like I always do and opened the back door to put my briefcase in. And out of nowhere this guy grabs me from behind and pushes me headfirst into the back seat and pins me down. I had a box full of stuff in the back seat, stuff meant for the Sally Ann. So I manage to reach into the box and grab my old iron. I swing it behind me as hard as I can, and I hit the guy right in the side of the head with it. Blood everywhere! He jumps out of the car holding his face, screaming his head off, and this other guy—must have been his partner or something—is just standing there stunned. So I start swinging it at him, and he runs around to the other side of the car. So I chase him with it like a crazy person. Then I get caught up in the cord and he slips into the driver's seat. I don't know how he got my keys but he ends up starting my car. At that point I'm hysterical, and he's really scared, and he keeps trying to get the car into gear. I must have hit the window five times before he took off in reverse— Almost ran over his friend. And before I could do anything, the other one jumps in and they're gone. Left me standing there with nothing but this old iron and blood all over my clothes.

(She cheers with the iron.) Yeah, here's to my health.

Erin Shields is a Toronto-based playwright and actor who won the 2011 Governor General's Award for her play, *If We Were Birds*. She trained in acting at the Rose Bruford College of Speech and Drama in London, England, and is a founding member of Groundwater Productions through which she creates, develops, and produces much of her work. *If We Were Birds* garnered two Dora Mavor Moore Awards for its Tarragon Theatre production and has since been translated into French, German, and Italian. Other plays include *Soliciting Temptation, Montparnasse,* and *Gilgamesh.*

If We Were Birds is a shocking, uncompromising examination of the horrors of war, giving voice to a woman long ago forced into silence, and placing a spotlight on millions of female victims who have been silenced through violence. When King Pandion marries his daughter Procne off to war hero King Tereus, she must leave her beloved sister Philomela behind. After years of isolation in a foreign land, Procne begs Tereus to collect her sister for a visit. When confronted with Philomela's beauty, Tereus's desire triumphs over reason, igniting a chain of horrific events.

Premiered at Tarragon Theatre, Toronto, in April 2010, in association with Groundwater Productions.

• • •

Back in the palace, PROCNE *removes her disguise, revealing herself to her sister Philomela.*

PROCNE

Sister. Sister.

I didn't know.
I didn't know.

I knew he needed…
I knew he had to…
I thought there was a difference between family and war.
I'm sorry.
I'm so sorry.

Listen to me.
Listen with those ears that heard
the screams of your ravaged tongue.
Tears won't help us.
Prayers won't help us.
Nothing but the sword will help us,
the sword or something worse,
if it can be found, then something worse to punish him
for this merciless attack.

Look at me, Sister.
Look at me with those eyes
that have watched the blood stream from your body.
I am as hard as rock, as unflinching as iron
and nothing will prevent me from inflicting
such enormous pain upon that tyrant, Tereus.

That name, it burns in my mouth and throat
and I cannot spit it out.
I will break his bones one by one,
stick needles through his swollen joints,
and hack away at his limbs,
chopping, or twisting, or burning.

I'll hang him from his tongue
like a fish on a hook
and let him dangle till the weight of it
sends him plummeting to earth,
until his soul is screaming, unhinged
and desperate for the underworld.
And I will follow him everywhere, torturing.
Torturing.

Feel me, Sister.
Feel the strength in these arms
that once held Tereus gently, but now pulse with wrath.
Hear the resolve of these lips:
this revenge will make the very earth gape in horror.

NED DICKENS
SEVEN

As a playwright, Ned Dickens's stage credits include the seven-play cycle *City of Wine* of which this play, *Seven*, is the last, *Beo's Bedroom*, *Icara*, *The Star Child*, and *Horse*. He taught high school for seven years, as well as creative writing at St. Lawrence College, and has served as playwright-in-residence at the National Theatre School and at Nightswimming Theatre, among others. Ned lives in Kingston, Ontario, where he crafts multi-media scripts for museums and science centres with Show Communications.

Throughout *City of Wine* seven unnamed characters persist. They are a response to the idea of Chorus: a shifting social matrix intended to represent the city itself. They are identified in the scripts, but never on stage, by object titles, like Bowl. The character not named Bowl is a major through line of the entire one-hundred-and-fifty-year story. He is part of an archetypal heritage that includes Jack Falstaff and Norm from the TV show *Cheers*.

In *Seven*, the unnamed are all that remains of Thebes. They run an open-air tavern/brothel in the Greek camp at the siege of Troy. They have, for absurd reasons, been ordered on a pointless mission at dawn which will leave them, and all memory of their great city, dead. They drink, squabble, and struggle to find some way to make their shared story survive and matter.

Premiered at Theatre Passe Muraille in May 2009 as part of the City of Wine Student Festival. *Seven* was commissioned and developed by Nightswimming Theatre.

● ● ●

BOWL

We will not die alone, for all of Thebes will die with us.
Look at those men out there, asleep, or dead.
What makes us different from them?
Not that we die tomorrow,
For every day, for ten long years, that has been true for
some of them.
It is true now.
Not that we know, for when a soldier goes to war
Part of him always is prepared to die.
In fact, until tonight, we were alone in this great camp.
We never fought the Trojans and we never faced our
own mortality.
So, now we do, and we are one with them, no more.
What makes this fire a different colour from the rest,
What makes we seven here unique,
Is that we speak the last words of a noble state.
I will do now a thing most terrible,
A thing I never in my life have done before.
Stand back and hold your loved ones tight.
I will, tonight, spill wine.

He does.

I am not mad or feverish,

Though I admit I shake a bit just now.

See how the wine, once spilled, is lost into the thirsty
dust,

Returned now, as it were, into the earth from which
it came?

Thebes has, for us, a long time now, enjoyed that other
name

"City of Wine."

The great god Bacchus, so the story goes,

Gave wine to us and we have shared it with the world.

It fires and flavours everything we do:

Each meal and every ritual,

A royal wedding or an old friend's memory.

It feeds our stories and it sparks our fights.

It is our blood, our sweat, our tears, our breath.

It cools our days and warms our darkest nights.

It marks our birth and bathes us after death.

I could go on and on.

I have.

Wine is the memory of Thebes.

We seven are the cups and bottles and the bowls that
hold it now.

Tomorrow we will all be shattered on the ground.

It is a loss of no significance to break a bottle,

But the wine, the wine is everything.

I say we sing the song of Thebes in seven voices, loudly
as we can,
Pour out our city's story to the thirsty night,
And hope that, somehow, some of it just might
Be caught and saved in other cups,
And tasted then on other lips.
A hundred thousand men, a thousand ships,
The greatest gathering the world has ever seen sur-
rounds us now,
Let us make them our audience
And give them Thebes.

BLUE

DAWN DUMONT
FANCYDANCER

Dawn Dumont is of Cree and Metis descent and grew up on the Okanese First Nation, located in Saskatchewan.

Fancydancer is a dark comedy based in Regina, Saskatchewan, about the disappearance and murder of Aboriginal women in Canada. The play begins when April Fineday, a 28-year-old Cree fancydancer and single mother, goes missing. Valerie Night, an ambitious journalist, searches for her by interviewing April's family and friends. In the process of her investigation, Valerie brings April's spirit back to earth from limbo. Once back, spirit April convinces Valerie to help her to bring her killer to justice.

The following monologue is the opening of the play which had a staged reading at the Two Worlds Festival in New Mexico in spring 2010.

• • •

APRIL walks on stage wearing a pair of sneakers, a red shirt and jeans, and one long, dangling turquoise earring.

APRIL

I always liked horror movies because the whole time you're watching them, you're second-guessing what the victim does. Don't leave the party to go have sex with your boyfriend. Don't go find out what that strange sound was. And never, ever go camping. But they never listen. Next thing you know the monster is after them and what do they do? Freeze and scream. And you're in front of the screen yelling: "Run, you dumb bitch, run! Pick up your feet! Kick off those dumb heels! And stop your fucking crying!" And then, of course, what does she do? She trips! Idiot!

We blame her. Or him; sometimes it's a guy being hacked to death. We don't blame the killer. I mean we picked the movie because we know he kills. That's his job. Can't blame him. So that just leaves... that bonehead in the halter top and short shorts. We feel for her when she dies—we think, aw that's too bad—no more sex scenes and boob shots.

After she dies, who's left? The cute guy and the virgin. The cute guy has about a fifty-fifty chance, but we all know the virgin's gonna beat the killer because she's smart. She wears glasses. She has small tits. Fucking ridiculous. But we all believe it. The virgin deserves to live. I don't know why—she's gotta be the most boring bitch in the movie and, personally, I'd rather hang out with the blonde—she looks like someone who knows how to party. But that's how movies are. That's how life is. If you have sex, then you're gonna pay for it.

When I was getting killed, I remember thinking at one moment— fuck, this is just like a movie. Except this blood is real and nobody is going to call cut and I'll never get to go to a movie premiere. Shitty.

It happened in a field outside the city and the last thing I saw was the stars filling up the whole sky—they didn't make me feel better about being killed—stars aren't much of a fucking consolation after getting the shit kicked out of you and having someone use you as a knife sharpener. But they were nice. All my life I've liked looking at them. It always looks like they're winking at you. Yeah those stars were nice.

By the way, I didn't know I was going to die. I thought—at least he's gone—now I'll just rest for a bit and then I'll get up and go get help. I was a little worried cuz I couldn't feel parts of me but at least my heart was still beating—I think I actually said, thank God my heart is still beating— Fuck, that's sad. *(laughs)*

I want you to know that I ran my ass off. As soon as that car door opened, I fucking ran. I'm no track star but I can move. But he could run faster. Then he tackled me around the waist and boom! I hit my head on a rock. That still pisses me off—of all the fucking bad luck. So then I started throwing punches but blood is flowing into my eyes. Probably turned him on with all that blood. I went for his eyes but he dodges me like a boxer and I remember thinking, "Ah, he's done this before."

Broke my cheekbone. Knocked some teeth free. And my nose—I always loved my nose, a gorgeous Indian nose—always looks good in pictures. After my nose broke, things got a lot harder: do you know how hard it is to breathe with a broken nose and a mouth full of blood?

I'm glad I fought. My mom used to tell me, when you're dealing with a bully, it ain't important whether you win or lose—it's only important that they know they fought you. So I went down hard—and that makes me feel a bit better. I always thought of myself as a tough little bitch and I should die like that.

I know what you're thinking—and yes I'm getting to it. Does your life pass before your eyes? Yup. And not to brag, but it's pretty awesome. Because it's not the crappy parts like when you had the flu or someone called you a dirty Indian or when you got arrested—it's the best parts—like laughing with my sister, or making love with someone you really care about, or holding my baby. And they're not just memories—it's like you're right there inside of them. The last thing I felt was the weight of my daughter's body in my arms, her little head right against my heart, smelling like baby powder and clean laundry and y'know... that baby smell. And I thought: life was so good to me.

Except for that last really shitty part.

APRIL saunters off the stage.

Lisa Codrington is an actor and writer based in Toronto. Her writing includes *Last Call*, *The Colony*, *Cast Iron*, and *Skylar*. *Cast Iron* is published by Playwrights Canada Press and was nominated for a Governor General's Literary Award for Drama. Her work has also been published in *Rattling the Stage*, *Beyond the Pale*, *Canadian Theatre Review*, and *Acting Out*. She has been playwright-in-residence at the Canadian Stage Company, Theatre Direct, Nightwood Theatre, and the Blyth Festival. Lisa was born in Winnipeg, Manitoba, and holds a B.A. in Criminology from the University of Manitoba and a B.F.A. in Acting from Ryerson University.

The Aftermath follows Jane, a self-taught lecturer determined to prepare as many people as possible for an environmental apocalypse. On the surface, she is a sharp and witty speaker, boldly presenting a set of homemade rules and lessons she believes to be crucial for survival. But beneath the bravado is the pain and resentment of someone desperately seeking control of an unpredictable world that has already claimed her son.

Presented as a work in progress at the LabCab Festival at Factory Theatre, Toronto; the rock.paper.sistahz festival (b current); the Groundswell Festival (Nightwood Theatre); and FemFest (Sarasvàti Productions).

• • •

JANE stands beside a flip chart and boom box. She holds markers and a pointer that she uses to illustrate and accentuate the points of her lecture. The entire set-up fits into the large duffle bag behind her. This is a lecture that can be set up and struck in minutes. JANE speaks to the audience.

JANE

It's like this, SOME SERIOUS APOCALYPTICAL SHIT IS ABOUT TO HIT THE FAN and if you fuckers are prepared it's a win-win for me. Means I don't have to worry about you jacking my goods, beggin me for help when it all goes down. Getting all unruly cause you don't know what to do. No thanks. I'd rather teach you. Cause it's like my dad always said, "Life's not about two times two. It's about YOU, my sweet baby Jane. YOU doing what you gotta DO to GET THROUGH." See?

Close your eyes. Just for a sec… and listen.

JANE turns on the boom box. Sounds of rain and thunder play.

Now, your mom ever tell you— I didn't say open 'em. *(pause)* Now, your mom ever tell you that when it rains God is crying? Well I'm here to tell you that when THE APOCALYPTICAL SHIT HITS THE FAN, it's gonna feel like God is bawling, and as a result we're gonna be falling. We're not gonna be able to put THIS on layaway or pray, pray for the "rain rain to go away" cause IT ain't comin back no other day. We're 'bout to get a TEMPEST that's locked, loaded, and ready

to assault. And once landfall is made, our DEBTS are gonna HAVE
to be PAID!

JANE turns off the boom box.

Now a Temp-EST (you can open 'em up again), a Temp-EST (NOT to
be confused with a temp-TRESS) is— ...and I'm ONLY explaining this
cause I don't want you to all go home thinkin *(imitating audience)*
"Temptress? She musta been talkin about my girl Janet!"

Uh, NO I'm talkin about a TEMPEST. You know, Shakespeare, *(quot-
ing Shakespeare)* "Hell is empty and..."

Anyway, a TEMPEST (for you laymen, that's a BIG HONKIN STORM)
is the shit hittin fan shit we gotta worry about. It's kinda like
what God laid down in the time of Noah. You know wind, rain,
flooding... the-ultimate-weapon-of-mass-destruction— *(pause)*
Okay so, some of you heathens in the back are looking at me like
you don't know what the fuck I'm talking about. In a nutshell:
God-got-pissed-cause-humans-were-being-all-human-like, so-he-
flooded-everything-'cept-for-goody-two-shoes-Noah, his-old-lady,
I-think-his-kids-maybe, and-a-couple-animals-and-birds-and-shit.
After everything, God felt bad and promised Noah that he wasn't
ever gonna do anything like that again. And then he also invented
rainbows, to like really, REALLY say sorry. Got it? Good.

Now, I don't wanna call God a liar, I'm sure he MEANS to keep
his promise and not flood us again BUT with all the hurricanes,
tsunamis, and monsoons all over the place... you gotta wonder if

maybe Mother Nature's got the reins. I mean she's the one taking the knocks while God gets all the props. If I were her, can't say I wouldn't unleash the biggest and baddest tempest THERE NEV-ER EVER WAS on our asses. She's got REASON to be pissed. Would you want someone to go and suck all the oil outta your CORE and then spill it all over your ocean FLOOR. *(imitating fuckin-non-coaster-usin-klutzes)* "We wanna building a pipeline" AKA LANDMINE you-fuckin-non-coaster-usin-klutzes!

God may be the alMIGHTY but that don't mean he's no AphroDITE. He ain't gonna be able to talk Mother Nature down… cause when you're that close to the EDGE…
It's like, "No disrespect, God, but forget YOU and your PLEDGE, I'M AH JUMPIN OFFA THIS ledge!"

Shift.

Look at Katrina. When that bayou bitch broke wind, nobody even had a nose to hold cause she snapped and scattered every last thing halfway between there and God knows where. People used to for-ty-degree weather and drinkin in the street, where every corner's got a kid with a horn have now come forth to live up north. Now they spend their days like the rest of us, shivering at the corner of Fuck Me It's Cold Crescent and Why The Hell Didn't I Buy Those Boots Boulevard… ONLY to have that TRIPTYCH trollop Sandy piss all over the Eastern Seaboard. Yeah man. Shit be getting together and causing havoc. So if that trip to Japan's not in your budget… no worries, just get your ass over to the West Coast and wait. Cause fuckin earthquakes and tsunamis be shipping shit from one side of the planet to the next. It may not be the Japan you want but Mother Nature never claimed to be no travel agent.

She works the line and has been for the last gazillion years without so much as a bathroom break. So is it any surprise that she's gone on strike?

And the thing is she ain't an essential service so THEY can't legislate her ass back to work.

Bottom line, YOU gotta take care of yourself, cause no one can protect you from Mother Nature's wrath but you.

Just take a look around. Every last thing requires "some" assembly. It's SELF-HELP THIS or SELF-SERVE THAT—I mean, why do we gotta PUMP our OWN GAS? Are we trained in handling flammable substances? Cause last time I checked, I was a factory defect soaked in sparks and saturated with the impulse to explode!

So, when the Tempest hits, don't expect your government to be there for you,
cause in the hours of 1 to 72,
they expect you to fend for yourself.
It's all right there on the website.

Only thing they're offering to get you through those first three days is w-w-w-dot downloadable run of the mill, food-water-shelter, stop-drop-and-roll, emergency guide buuuuullshit dot-com.
Even after that I wouldn't be counting down the hours till "rescue."

Look what happens when a couple inches of snow falls
or the subway stalls
or parts of the expressway fall down
or kids get bored in the "bad" part of town
and shoot up a party.
Rescue and repair are often tardy.
Now sure, we had that one-day-blackout-on-that-warm-August-
night and it was cool.
Meant silence and ice cream for dinner
but if that were to go on for one day more…
…and more
        …and more

        Beat.

It'll be just like Katrina,
'cept we'll be stored in some shitty hockey arena,
and instead of cheering the fights on the ice
we'll be battling each other for two grains of uncooked rice
NEVER MIND having to dodge the rats and mice.

But "Oh no" you say,
"Katrina was so long ago
and it didn't even happen here
so really, we got nothing to fear."

Except for mudslides, avalanches, earthquakes, tsunamis, and lost
hockey games out west; forest fires, tornadoes, and floods in the

middle; nuclear disaster, hurricanes, badass drivers, and fucked up
mayors in the east. And up north… well they already know.

So watch out,
cause if you're poor
rotten to the core
or a huge chore
or an alternate couleur
or live a life many abhor,
when IT hits
you're not gonna get much more
than a COT and as far as you can spread your arms left to right.

Cause as SOON as you TAKE their "REF-UGE" you're a ref-u-gee,
and then they start treating you like a pes-ky flee.
Separating mother and daughter,
and son from father.
It's only the lucky ones who get reunited at the airport, cameras all
jammed in their faces. Most folks end up wandering the streets till
the end of time with nothing more than a hand drawn picture of
their loved ones.

Or it's like you see on those TV specials about the WORST OF WORLDS.
Where sorry suckers with flies in their eyes get shuffled off to a soc-
cer stadium, and then AS SOON as their foot hits the pitch *(imitating
a gun)* POW POW POW POW POW

That's why I say fuck self-doubt.
Let's carve our own route.

Saddle up and ride this Tempest out.

And yeah, TV's gonna SAY, "Little ole you can't save the day so don't
STAY.
Pack up the kids and get on the highway."
But whoa whoa whoa…
What good is contraflow
when there's no PLACE to go?

Don't get me wrong, it's gonna be one hell of a bout,
with very little twist and shout
BUT I PROMISE, if you listen to what I relay
all yuh all and me, we're gonna to be able to keep this Tempest at bay
while all the rest of these jokers end up fish fillet and liver pâté on
Mother Nature's lunch tray!

   Shift.

So, the first thing you gotta know, is that HUMANITY just GETS IN
THE WAY of survival. So forget alla that "pardon me" and "after you"
bullshit. I know it's hard. I mean, there are still times when I catch
myself using "sorry" for everything from "excuse me" to "look, hey,
I don't wanna see your face no more." It's a daily struggle, but if you
work at it, it's gonna pay off when the time comes.

I mean, I've come far. Like, you shoulda seen me back when all the
kids in the neighbourhood started getting the chicken pox. Now,
I've always been one to be ready, so anytime calamine was on sale,
I'd buy a bottle cause I knew the chicken pox were coming, and

when the epidemic hit I didn't want to be caught with my pants down. Told all the other mothers too, but do you think any of them bothered to prepare?

Oh no.

Nobody listens to Janie. But next thing you know, *(imitating Debbie)* "Hi Jay it's Debbie. I hear you got extra calamine."

OF COURSE Debbie's son Abraham is the first to go down. So what do I go and do? Stupid me goes and gives her every last bottle like I'm running a fuckin relief centre. Next thing you know Debbie's all *(imitating Debbie)* "I'm havin a pox party and everyone's invited."

So, thanks to DEBBIE and her son ABRAHAM, every kid on the block got a pox, EXCEPT (surprise-surprise) for MY Benny. Debbie's all *(imitating Debbie)* "I'd invite you in, but we already have so many kids here and... I don't want Abraham to feel overwhelmed. You understand right?"

Still I can't totally blame Debbie

...that kid of hers... *(imitating Abraham)* "I don't want Benny at my party. He's weird."

Fuckin Abraham!

With a name like that he should have SEEN Benny needed the chicken pox JUST AS BAD if not WORSE that any of those other snot-nosed bastards. He shoulda BEGGED Benny to come to his pox party. He should have LAID HANDS on my son and got his suffering over and done—

AH, what do I know... I can't remember who the hell Abraham was. I mean I know he BEGAT somebody in the beginning of the Bible but then after that...

…actually part of me's glad Benny didn't go.

I mean, there wasn't nothing but vertical STRIPEs in that house. Sit on Debbie's couch long enough and you feel like you're behind bars. Seriously, they were everywhere, on the curtains, on the lampshades, the dishes… even on the walls—

WHICH was against the rules. You'd nail up a couple pictures and they were ready to evict.

But some folks gotta ACT like they OWN their "townhouse" never mind they got less than a church mouse.

I mean when your housing is subsidized and your husband sells burgers and fries…?!

You gotta keep an eye out for the Debbies of this world. They're the bitches that spend half their life tryin to reach their target heart rate BEFORE even checking to see if they STILL have a heart. That being said they got their humanity in check and you gotta admire that. Debbie knew full well everything starts with the chicken pox.

DAVID YEE
CARRIED AWAY ON THE CREST OF A WAVE

David Yee was born and raised in Toronto. He is Hapa, of Scottish and Chinese descent. In addition to being a playwright, Yee is an actor and Artistic Director of fu-GEN Asian Canadian Theatre Company.

A press conference at the International Earth Rotation and Reference System Service, Australia.

Premiered at Tarragon Theatre, Toronto, in April 2013.

THE LEAP SECOND STORY

BECKETT, a scientist in a lab coat, enters. She has a tablet computer that she refers to as she presents. The reporter with whom she shared a moment earlier in her day is in the audience.

BECKETT

Ladies and gentlemen of the press. *(beat)* Especially gentlemen. *(beat)* Especially the gentleman in the blue coat who passed me in line earlier and brushed my shoulder and we both turned because a wave of electricity passed through us that was something like the feeling when you drink milk that's gone off, only good, and neither of us spoke but I wanted to tell you that you are the handsomest man I think I've ever seen. *(beat)* Thank you for joining us.

Clears her throat.

People often ask me what it is we do at the International Earth Rotation and Reference Systems Service. I think it's rather self-explanatory, but that's me. Over the years of being asked this question, I've simplified my explanation to the following statement: We observe.

This may blow your mind, but the Earth changes speed and position, constantly. Over the course of centuries the mean Earth day has gotten longer, then shorter, then longer again. A number of factors are responsible for this. For instance:

On December 26, 2004, the earth's mass was drawn towards its core via tectonic subduction and the planet got… smaller. Because the planet got smaller, it started to spin faster, three microseconds faster than before. The day got shorter. But the force also tilted the planet, 2.5 centimetres on its axis. It wobbled. Like knocking a spinning top, the tidal shifts created a "drag" effect, slowing us back down. The day got longer. These differences in microseconds may seem infinitesimal at the moment… but they *do* add up.

We, as scientists, as observers of anomalous planetary behaviour, as record keepers of the "big picture," must account for these shifts and their impact on the future of our world. Like balancing a ledger, we—the accountants of time—have instituted necessary measures to maintain our pace with the Earth. About every eighteen months, we add a leap second to Coordinated Universal Time. You aren't aware of it. But it's there. Inserted into the fabric of your day.

And by a marvel of science, a breakthrough in observatory technology that would take far longer to explain than we have tonight… for the first time ever: I can tell you what happened in that leap second. That fraction of a glimmer of the mere concept of a moment. You didn't even notice it. Because you weren't watching. But we were watching. And we wanted to let you all know… because if you know… then maybe we stand a chance after all. What happened in the leap second went something like this:

A balloon burst at a child's birthday party.
A mosquito pierced the surface of my skin.
Twelve people laughed at the same joke.

A plane lifted from the ground.

Two strangers shared a glance across a crowded subway car.

A match was struck to light a cigarette.

You smiled at me.

A phone rang once.

A honeybee disappeared into thin air.

Six people standing together all experienced déjà vu.

My face flushed at the sight of you.

A supercomputer finished calculating the end of pi.

A grasshopper swallowed a garden snake.

The Internet crashed.

Every child alive stopped crying.

California caught on fire.

There was peace on Earth.

We fell in love.

The world ended.

And we were all reborn.

> BECKETT *puts the tablet down. She steps off the stage and into the audience. She finds the reporter in the blue jacket. She stands him up, and kisses him.*

TAWIAH M'CARTHY
THE KENTE CLOTH

Tawiah M'Carthy is a Ghanaian-born, Toronto-based theatre artist. His playwriting credits include *Obaaberima* and *The Kente Cloth*.

The Kente Cloth is a multidisciplinary play that tells the heartfelt story of a young gay man from Ghana who is preparing to marry his Canadian–Scottish fiancé. It's the big day and the Scotsman is putting on his kilt, but with an unexpected visitor from the past, the young Ghanaian is struggling to wear his kente cloth. *The Kente Cloth* explores one man's process of compartmentalizing family and tradition from his old home into one bowl and the expectations of his new home in another.

It's hours before his wedding and the groom is grappling with whether to say, "I do" as William Victor Osei-Pearson or Nana Oto Kwabena Adjei. After you've run from who you are and where you're from, how do you find your way back?

The Kente Cloth premiered at the SummerWorks Theatre Festival, Toronto, in 2008. Produced by (plural productions).

• • •

WILL-VIC

I loved my names growing up and I still do, it was different, it was cool… at least that was what everyone said.
William Victor Osei-Pearson, that was for school and paperwork.
Nana Oto Kwabena Adjei was for home and family.
And to those who did not know me… my name, I was the son of Dr. Osei-Pearson.

I loved being the "son of…"
I believed if they saw me as that, there must be something of him they saw in me.
Being the "son of…" made me as wise, strong, loved, and respected as him; my father.

It took away my faults.
I was the "son of…"

I wanted to be just like him.
A man with strength, wit, charm, and pride.

I have my father's eyes and ears,
I have my father's nose and lips,
I have my mother's skin, I carry my mother's spirit
Yes, I am the son of…
I opened the door to a face I had forgotten

There he stood, no tears, no smiles, a face that grew
up, out from my past
My legs begun to shake
I was seeing a ghost.
There he was. Here, looking at me.

Dadaa!

He came in. He took a seat.
I did not have much to say, but he did.
He spoke, I listened,
He spoke and spoke and spoke, of his work, his garden,
my brothers, my sisters, he sang of Mamaa…
And then he asked of you.
He wanted to know how you, an *obroni, (a white man)*
and me, an *obibini, (a black man)* can do this.
So I spoke.
I spoke of you…
I spoke of us.

Aaron Bushkowsky has been produced and published in several genres: film, poetry, theatre, prose, and non-fiction. His book of poetry, *ed and mabel go to the moon*, was nominated for the Dorothy Livesay Poetry Prize. Aaron has also been nominated for Vancouver's Jessie Richardson Theatre Awards for Outstanding Original Play eight times over the past thirteen years, more than any other playwright in Canada, winning two. As a dramaturg and story editor, Aaron has worked on over fifty plays and a number of film scripts. Other books include a collection of short stories titled *The Vanishing Man*, *Strangers Among Us,* and *The Waterhead*, three plays produced by Solo Collective, a theatre company he helps run. His latest published drama is *My Chernobyl*.

A developer is charged with the murder of a social activist in a riveting tale of intrigue involving big business and real estate. A whodunit with a twist as we piece together divergent scenes that eventually lead us to the killer.

   Darren is a big-city lawyer who has never lost a case, but he is now asked to consider taking on a strange harassment case by a shady developer in the middle of one of the biggest real estate deals of the year.

Premiered at Performance Works, Vancouver, in April 2004, produced by Rumble Theatre.

• • •

DARREN (forties) is in BOB's office. Light knifes through the slats in the blinds. BOB is in the dark nearby.

DARREN

So, a woman is bothering you at work? She comes and goes as she pleases. She has no respect for your privacy or your personal space. She threatens to stop the development. Stop the development? Stop the development? Well, I think we have a case for harassment, don't you? I can make this work, don't you worry. It doesn't matter how huge your company is, or how wealthy you are. I've defended some of the biggest banks in the business and if you knew how much they screwed you, you wouldn't want them to win. Check your statement lately? Who does, right? A buck here, a buck there. Whatever. As long as it's convenient. Anyway, long story short, I've never lost a case because I never give people a choice between good or bad. Not about that. It's about the thin line between. A truth all of its own. And that, my friend, is what we can get away with. Think about Woody Allen, mid-career Woody, not washed-up weirdo Woody doing old-guy comedy with young nubile women one-third his age. Jesus. *(beat) Crimes and Misdemeanors…* God, that was so full… what you can get away with. And truth and there are many paths to the truth or away from it. And really, that's the cool thing about being a lawyer. We're actually filmmakers. We just paint a picture… we dabble in the grey areas: we show how people can be fragile and confused, and let's say, disconnected. We all are. Come on, life is difficult, right? A man sits in his empty kitchen, a bare light bulb over his head. He is broken, sobbing… things are piling up, bills, bills, bills. He hasn't slept in days. He's about to lose his job and he is *exactly* like us.

A shell of a man. Crumbling into dust. Who could blame him?

I love movies. If I wasn't a lawyer. I'd be making movies. Good movies always have moral dilemmas. Good people do bad things, that sorta element. But things are changing, right? Sometimes it pisses me off. Didn't movies used to be about "Do I trust this person?" then suddenly they changed to "Do I trust what's going on?" and now they're "Do I trust *me*, my own perceptions?" What happened? *(beat)* Even in our dreams we've become paranoid narcissists, haven't we?

So, where does that leave us?

Well, I want you to notice, I didn't say "enlightenment." I would never say that. Never. More than ever it's just about how we live and what we do, not why. And that's exactly why I practice law.

An actor–writer–director born and raised in Tabora, Tanzania, Joan M. Kivanda is a graduate of the theatre program at the University of Guelph and b current's rAiz'n the sun ensemble program. Her performance poetry, *a beautiful friendship*, has been featured at the AfriCanadian Playwright Festival and Vancouver's UrbanInk Productions while her performance work has appeared at festivals like rock.paper.sistahz, the Fringe, SummerWorks, Writenow!, and Luminato. Her directing work has included *Who the Hell is Eleanor, Oh Sudanna*, and *This is a Play*, as well as working as an assistant on *Binti's Journey, Scratch, The Polished Hoe, Seussical the Musical*, and *Wise.Woman*.

Stori ya maintains a culturally specific narrative about an African-Canadian woman born in a small village in Tanzania as she attempts to hold on to her Africanness. Maria Msondo delivers a swelling chorus of anecdotes as she invites us to her small-town Canadian house for the "last supper." As the clock ticks and the tension builds, Maria fills our ears with the journey of her life, as hard as it has been, culminating in tales of a childhood that is full of tragedy and heartbreak.

Maria drifts in and out of her past, sometimes playing the past, sometimes immersed in the past, sometimes telling stories of the past. Whenever she is engaged in a conversation, she becomes that age or that person as she *remembers* them.

Premiered at Harbourfront's HATCH, Toronto, 2005.

• • •

MARIA

I don't trust people.

Everybody wants something from me
Everybody
All they do is take take take—

I have given and given and given and got nothing in
return.

I have worked so hard in my life—so hard—and nobody has helped me. I have been everywhere, to all
second-hand stores in town. The Salvation Army, St.
Vincent, Second Look, Value Village, Goodwill, all of
them. I searched everywhere for cheap fridges, cook-
ers, shoes, clothes, computers, cameras… I filled my
container over and over again, shipped it to Tanzania
with Bob, hoping to turn my life around, but every
time it got there, it was always the same. My good-for-
nothing family would line up, their hands in front of
them, begging begging begging…

VOICE #1

Auntie, I need *hela za sadaka*, for church.

VOICE #2

Mama, *naomba gauni mpya.* For graduation. I want to look my best.

MARIA

What do they think? I'm a millionaire.

VOICE #3

Shangazi, I was just wondering if you could help me with tuition. You know my father is sick, they think it's AIDS, my mother is taking care of my little sister, I really need your help.

VOICE #4

What's up, Auntie? What did you bring this time-ya, I got a new girlfriend-ya, I want to give her something totally cool-ya?

VOICE #5

Dada, dada, *za Kanada*, dada? *Ninulie bia basi*, come on, dada, just one *bia*.

MARIA

Dada dada. Auntie, Shangazi. *Ma mkumbwa. Ma mdogo.*
Everybody wants something.
I have given them everything!
Everything and they ask for more!

I can't give any more.

I'm in debt.
The Visa cards are after me. The American Express.
The MasterCard. The mortgage.
They are coming to take my house away.

They're on their way.
What time is it?
Oh, I can't lose it now.

What time is it?
This is my house
I need a little time, just a little time...

What time is it?

What time is it?

Oh my God...
Mungu wangu, Mungu wangu, jamani
Mungu wangu uko wapi?
Oh my God... They are coming
Jamani, jamani jamani,
Nyumba yangu-nyumba yangu jamani
Wananyanganya nyumba yangu leo.
They are coming.

No No No
They are taking my house away.

This is my house.
I have paid for this house
I have paid with my blood.
I have been humiliated, used, abused, punished in this house.

My name is written all over the wall.
Maria, Maria, Maria, Maria, Maria, Maria!
This is my house.
Hii ni nyumba yangu
Kutoka kwa babu yangu.

I'm glad you are here
I'm very glad you could come.
This is my house.
A present from my grandfather.

I'm glad you are here.
They cannot take my house away from me.
No–no-no.
This is my house.
They cannot take it away.
I'm glad you are here.
I'm very glad you could come.

Tell them you live here.
Tell them you pay rent.
Tell them you live here.

I'm very glad you could come,
Nashukuru, nashukuru sana.

My husband took my soul. He took my life. My confidence. He took everything from me except this house.

I have paid for this house.
Mwenyezi Mungu anajua,
I have paid for this house

They have taken everything from me.
Everything.
I do not have a place I call home,
But I have this house, this house
I will not give it away.
Not to the bank.
Not to anybody.

No
I will not give it to my good-for-nothing family,
They have done nothing for me.

You have done nothing for me.

I will not give it to you because you are here.

No!

I will not give it to you because you are black like
me. Nonono. No. Not anymore. I have given enough.
Enough. I have stayed away from you all. I have stayed
away. No no no, I will not give it to you because you
are black like me. Not any more. I am not a part of
you. I am not like you. Yes, yes, I am from Africa, but
I'm not just an African, I am a Tanzanian. Not just a
Tanzanian, I am a Nyamwezi. Not just a Nyamwezi,
I am a Haya and a Nyamwezi. Not just a Haya and a
Nyamwezi. I am me. Me.

Me and me and me and me and me.

We are not a family.
I cannot give the house to you not even if...

I am not like you.

I have a father with seventeen children.
No, I don't know him. He doesn't know me. I don't
know his children.
No, I did not grow up with my mother or my aunt.
No, my grandmother did not teach me that.
No, I don't know that story.
I don't believe in magic.
I don't celebrate that.

Actually, my mother said to stay away from you.
You African-American, Caribbean-African,

African-Canadian—or whatever you call yourself. Diasporic African. You are not from Africa. You don't even know what Africa is like. You have never been there. You are disrespectful. You have no passion. You do drugs. You don't finish school. You kill each other. Nobody cares about you. Nobody. My mother said to stay away from you. You are a bad influence. I don't want to be like you.

See, this is my house. I keep my house clean. My neighbours don't want anybody else to stay here but me. I'm a good neighbour. Ask them. I am not like you. I keep a clean house. They like me. I plant flowers. Mow the lawn. This is my house. I am not like you. I don't want to be like you. I don't want any trouble.

I could have been a princess, did you know that?
Princess Maria
People would have respected me
I would have lived in a castle
People would have respected me

Princess Maria.

Lina lanye Maria. Maria *Msondo*. Msondo Maria. Maria…

I could have been a princess.

Waawaate Fobister is an award-winning actor, playwright, choreographer, dance, storyteller, and producer. A proud Anishinaabe from Grassy Narrows First Nation, he is a graduate of Humber College's Theatre Performance Program. After the success of *Agokwe*, Waawaate's second play, *Medicine Boy*, premiered at SummerWorks in 2012. He has performed in numerous plays including, but not limited to, *The Rez Sisters*, *A Very Polite Genocide*, *White Buffalo*, *Cafe Woman*, and *Death of a Chief*, and acted in the television series *The Time Travelers*. His most recent projects include the production of his play *Biiwidi-Stanger* as part of the Idle No More Wrecking Ball performance and as a dance in *I'm Not the Indian You Had in Mind*.

Agokwe explores the unrequited love between two teenage boys from neighbouring reserves. Mike, a hockey player, and Jake, a traditional dancer, notice each other at the Kenora Shoppers Mall and ultimately connect through a mutual love of movement. They meet briefly at a post-hockey-tournament party where they bashfully confess their desire for one other. But youth, distance, and isolation strive to pull the threads apart when tragedy intervenes.

Nanabush, the storyteller, opens the play, giving the audience some insight on the world as he sees it.

Agokwe premiered at Buddies in Bad Times Theatre in Toronto in September 2008.

• • •

NANABUSH

Hello! Good evening. Can you see me? You can see me, right? Of course you can see me. I am standing right in front of you, flesh and blood. But the only reason you can see me is because I choose for you to see me. Before you came in here *(points to someone in the audience)* I was the shithead who spilled coffee on you at the office. I was the old man with the hugest boner protruding through his pants on the street. A moment ago, I was the itch on the ring of your asshole as you sat down and took your seat. I am Nanabush. I am a trickster. I am the trickster, the trickster of tricksters.

The wings NANABUSH *is wearing pull away as he spins.*

So, let's just get straight to the point. I'm here to tell you something; something very important. Once you get it, I want you to act on it and tell your friends, and tell your friends to tell their friends, and tell their friends to tell their friends. That way we can all live together like a nice big happy family. Do you like living in a nice big happy family? I know I do. I mean, who wouldn't want to live in a nice happy family? Some of you are disagreeing with me. Why is that? Maybe your family is disgusting? Maybe every time when your family sits down to have a nice big meal someone always manages to fart, or burp, or choke, or argue until you want to die? Or is it just simply the fact that no one in your family gets along or understands you… or whatever the case is, the truth is, not everyone has a nice big happy family. You know why? Because humans are stupid. Stupid, I tell ya—they may be the smartest species on the planet, but they are also the stupidest. Not only that, they're also one of the most disgusting and despicable species around; makes me sick to my stomach. Sorry to give you the bad news but I am just being honest. They—you—yes you, you're gross. You dirty everything. Everything you get your filthy little hands on, it gets dirty—the land, the air, the water, and yourselves. Lost people, it's a shame. But I should give you some credit; you are trying to make things better. Everyone is trying to think green to save the planet, to save yourselves, but its not easy being green, or white, or yellow, or black, or Anishnaabe, red! That's why I am here to tell you about the Anishnaabe, my lost people. Their culture is disappearing, going fast. So many things have changed. So many things have been taken away from them: their land, their traditions, their freedom, and their sense of who they were and who they are. Oh, I know you have heard this all before. Poor Anishnaabe, why don't they just get off the bottle and get over it? I'll tell you why. Because once you've been screwed it's hard to unscrew yourself!! Oh… am I making you a little bit uncomfortable? Oh, I know I am not being the apologetic little Indian. Well, I don't give a shit because I am Nanabush. The truth isn't always pretty and it isn't easy. It took two hundred years for an apology and all they have to say is "I'm sooryyyyyyy"!! And what do you want me to say? "Oh oh, Mr. Harper, its okay. I will just go and find my little children's missing bones that're now part of this condo that just got built here." Well, we all know what's been done—man's inhumanity to man, tsk, tsk, tsk… like I said, you humans are stupid. All we got is the present and the future so let's make it a fabulous one.

Jon Lachlan Stewart has been writing plays since he was a kid. Credits include *Little Room*, *Grumplestock's*, *Twisted Thing*, *Big Shot*, *Dog*, *The Gooble Portrait*, and *Dirty Mouth*, as well as the upcoming *The Genius Code* and *Edith Rex*. Jon is the co-founder and artistic director of Surreal SoReal Theatre, with Vincent Forcier, in Edmonton. Surreal SoReal explores the darkness of contemporary urban stories, comic or dramatic, and creates new touring productions with an emphasis on physical theatre and the surreal. Jon is a graduate of Studio 58 in Vancouver, and is currently studying as a director at the National Theatre School in Montreal.

A boy witnesses a brutal shooting on the Vancouver SkyTrain. Fascinated by the spectacular, he's here, in the theatre, to *pitch* the event to you as a movie. The boy slides in and out of all the characters involved: the mother of the victim, a not-so-recovered heroin addict named Killiger, a seventy-year-old Japanese pickpocket named Odosung, and a gravelly police officer by the name of Byron. Each of these characters are involved in the tragedy, but none want to carry the blame.

A young boy with a love for movies. He's after something that feels real.

Premiered at the Toronto Fringe Festival in 2008.

• • •

BOY

I saw a terrible movie. It was so bad that it hurt. It was called *The Stop.*

So it's like this cardboard brick exposed like underbelly, like an IN-dependant theatre.

IN-dependant.

As in like *really* dependant on people being really pretentious cuz it's really bad.

Cuz everybody's like *dressed up* and there's actually people there who worked on the movie and you don't buy popcorn, you buy like—*English licorice*, which is supposed to be a step up from popcorn, but there's NO POPCORN IN THE MOVIE THEATRE. God.

So I'm watching the thing. And it's this girl and this guy and right away I'm like meeeeeeehhh but I stay there cuz going home is boring and it's this girl. Who rides the train all the time. And she has this shit job and a shit boyfriend and blah blah blah and she takes the same stop home every day and sees people, people watches. And then it's this guy. Who has a shit job and a shit girlfriend, etc., and rides the train every day blah blah blah and one day they see each other. And I'm like WHAT AN UNEXPECTED TWIST! And they can't love each other, because they have their shit boyfriend and girlfriend, and I'm like OMG, CONFLICT. And someone's brother is cheating on someone, someone has cancer, and I was too busy furiously hitting the giant cupholder to care—WHICH DOESN'T HAVE A DRINK BECAUSE DRINKS AREN'T ALLOWED BECAUSE THERE'S NO DRINKS IN THE THEATRE.

But anyway, it comes to this artsy moment? And they're the only ones on the train, and they're naked, and they're doing it, and there's music by some IN-dependant baaaand… and they're like parting their separate ways, and the doors of the SkyTrain open wide—

The BOY's *hands snap up to his face.*

And there's this crowd…

His hands frame his face as he pans the audience silently.

Pans.

This big…
Judging…
Crowd…
Witnesses.
Who all want it to stop, but it just *stays*

And then the train just moves on like nothing even happened.

A fast, dismissive snap back to the story.

Okaaay...

So they take this one moment which could've maybe, like MAYBE been interesting, and then they just throw it away. And it like *builds up* to this whole moment, and then they just have to stop seeing each other. Which is why it's called *The Stop*...?

(silently mouths the words) Oh my god...

And the only people who are going to like this are yuppies with MacBooks and square-framed glasses who are like: "Ode to Vancouver!"

This is what my grade six storylines get marked on! It's everything we want, every pretty little thing we *believe* makes real life interesting even though it's not: the lovers love each other, the police officer on the train *isn't* a corrupt prick, the boy's mom is like sick and dying so we have to pity her, and there's no train crashes or dying—there's no *tragedy*. Don't we want to see something that you can't expect? Wouldn't that give us something we can remember?

Don't we want a car crash in the middle of a bridge?
Don't we want a fire in the place across the street?
Don't we want a column sticking out on channel four?
Don't we like to sit and stop and stare at accidents?

YES. Yes. Stop me. Surprise me. Before I'm old.
When I get old I want scars. I want a story to tell.

Thirteen of Mansel's plays have been produced across the country. They include *Muskeg & Money*, *Thea*, *Bite the Hand*, *Picking Up Chekhov*, *Spitting Slag*, and *Street Wheat*. He has been writer-in-residence at the Berton House in Dawson City, Northern Light Theatre, the University of Windsor, the Regina Pubic Library, and the Surrey Public Library. *Two Rooms* won the 2010 John V. Hicks Award and the 2010 Uprising National Playwriting Award. Mansel was shortlisted for the 2011 Siminovitch Prize in Theatre for Playwriting. He lives in Chapleau, Northern Ontario.

Murdoch is a white cop who willingly confesses to the murder of his Muslim wife, Maha, to a pair of unseen policemen. Maha is a young Uyghur from the Muslim region of western China. Her confession, also to an unseen listener, takes place elsewhere, some time just before her murder. Her confession is rather more mundane: she has cheated on her husband.

Murdoch, middle-aged, is an aggressively smart and decent public servant. "How the hell did I get here?" is his question tonight. Maha, his wife, is maybe ten years younger. She's guilty and she feels it deeply, but she's not guilty as charged.

Two Rooms premiered at Persephone Theatre, Saskatoon, in April 2011. A French version, translated by Jean Marc Dalpé, was co-produced by Le Théâtre du Nouvel-Ontario, Sudbury, and Théâtre de la Vieille 17, Ottawa. It has been touring Eastern Canada since 2012.

• • •

A room.

MAHA

In this place, where strangers come and go, where strangers tell their secrets, perhaps to find a little peace, I think it might be easy to confess. I hope this is true. And I hope confession will bring comfort.

There is a man. Two men, in fact. Murdoch is the name of one. He is my husband. The other, his name is... I call him K. K is my confession. But I think Murdoch as well.

Two men, and fearful times.

I am at the airport. It is early morning. I know the young man at the X-ray machine, the man with the wand. He has seen me many times, and even more often this last year. He banters with me, his dull job, me always traveling. Just a nice young Sikh wearing a turban, a beautiful blue Dastar. I walk through the X-ray, the usual annoyance, you know what I mean, but he makes it bearable for both of us. "Maha, your passport, so full of stamps, like James Bond, like a woman of mystery." Jokes, banter, a kind of truth, though the young man in the Dastar does not know it is a kind of truth.

I am picking up my laptop. And I hear a muttering at my shoulder. A businessman, perhaps forty-five, good-looking, fit, successful. He says, "These people, they really stick together. Buddy-buddy in the turban, he barely searched her. I had to take my shoes off. My shoes, in my country, can't understand a single thing he says, I'm in my stocking feet and she waltzes through like she was walking in her own front door." The businessman turns to me, close, very close. "Why don't you people go back where you come from. Leave us in peace."

His hiss, peace, spittle on my cheek.

> *The other room.*
> *An interrogation light is on.*

MURDOCH

You can turn that off.

I'm prepared to talk.

C'mon fellas. This isn't 1943, this ain't Nazi Germany. And a light like that, it's straight outta *Hogan's Heroes*. Remember? Sergeant Schultz? "Nutink, I know nutink." No? Forget it.

We're in the middle of an energy crisis here fellas, held hostage to foreign oil. C'mon. How about a little respect for a fellow hostage? Or think of it this way—turn off the juice and your grandchildren will thank you for trying to save this shit storm of a climate.

Oh well. No hope for the climate anyway. As per usual, too little, too late, too bad, so sad. Western civilization really is too dumb to survive.

What's with you guys? I expected to spend tonight with a couple of professionals. Christ, did all the talented cops retire? Has the Rapture already arrived? Is it only me and you two left?

Well. You confess to the one that brung ya in, eh fellas. So pay attention and I will lead you in a master class on what a confession should look, smell, and feel like. From motive to execution. As it were. The facts, the feelings, the details. The intellectual social and spiritual background of a crime of—what's the word?—oh yeah, passion. The forensics. The weather. What the goddamn poodle had for breakfast on the day in question. You will have so much evidence even you clowns won't be able to botch the case. Okay? Now—the light?

Interrogation light off.

Thank you.

We begin.

Once upon a time, it was a dark and stormy night.

Interrogation light back on.

No sense of humour, eh fellas. I guess it's gonna be a long shift. But this confession, it'll get better, don't you fret. More personal.

Private even. I think. I don't know for sure. This is all very new to me. Usually, as you know, I'm on the other side of the table. And, just for the record? I'm a smart cop. My partner's smart too. My ex-partner. So if you think about a team as good cop/bad cop, one half brains, one half knuckle dragger, I guess that leaves your team one smart cop short, am I right?

Just kidding. Just the usual collegial banter. An icebreaker. Locker room BS: "How's your wife? She still smoking cigarillos in bed?"

Okay, okay.

Let's start by acknowledging the elephant in the room. My wife was a Muslim. Yes she was, my wife, my Maha, was a Muslim.

And while we're at it, let's acknowledge another elephant: we are at war. Yes we are. The war on terror.

One final elephant: I did kill my wife. Let's be terribly clear about that.

Interrogation light off.

MAHA

After we take off, a woman watches me open my laptop. She watches me. She stares. She has a glossy magazine in her hands but most of all she watches me. Her question is silent, her question is obvious, her question I have heard whispered a thousand times—my laptop—is it a bomb?

She stares at me.

I stare at my hands.

I never touch the keypad.

MURDOCH

That's an awful lot of elephants in such a small room fellas. Watch your step. Elephant dung piles up about two feet high.

Maha and I rode elephants in Thailand once. Though I preferred riding Mekhong Whisky. A rougher ride if I remember correctly.

You fellas might not know this but the south of Thailand is Muslim. Sort of like Mississauga but with better surfing.

Ah. Bigotry, racism even, racism rears its ugly head. Murdoch is a racist. Tsk tsk.

C'mon fellas, help me out here—admit, at least, that we live in a racist country. You know it and I know it. You can sit in a pub in the retirement towns up and down the west coast, and the only conversation you hear is some retired schoolteacher born in South Sodomy Warwickshire and some draft dodger outta Ku Klux Kentucky bitching about the immigrants. The brown immigrants of course cause if you're white you ain't an immigrant, you're as good as sliced bread and easy credit. We don't even like our own Indians—and they at least walked over the land bridge ten thousand years ago. So you think some Sikh been living here twenty years has a Chinaman's

Chance? Not in a country that only gives the Indian any muskeg swamp piece of no-good dirt the CPR couldn't make a dollar from. All I'm saying is oh yes, I come by my bigotry honestly.

And if the sheet fits I might as well wear it. I got a murder charge hanging around my neck, I guess I can wear a little bigotry too. But I'll tell you this: the war on terror is going to go on for a long, painful time. Your children's children will still be fighting this war. So look at me. Take a long hard look. This is what your children's children will look like. I am the future.

You don't like me fellas. And I'm gonna tell you why: you got this hang-up about remorse.

Let me tell you a little story about remorse.

I was green on the street and I get a call—shoplifter. Sounds funny now that cops are so busy we can't respond unless there's four dead and two dying but that's how it was back in the day. So I go, shoplifter's maybe seventeen, wet behind the ears, hitching cross-country, no money, no clue. He tells me his story—boo hoo, I'll never do it again, I was hungry, winge and whine. I toss him in the cell for the night, drag him upstairs for court the next morning—but I let him walk, maybe he's learned his lesson. Thank you, thank you, he says, grovel grovel. Couple years later I get a Christmas card from the kid, go figure—he's in law school, thanks for the break, Joyeux Noël. Every Christmas, thank you, thank you—till last year, I see in the paper he's up for a five million dollar fraud, walks on a technicality, gets to keep the five mill and the jet ski at the cottage, once a thief always a thief.

So as far as I'm concerned: remorse—useless information.

But here's the real moral of the story: my remorse, my business.

SHAHIN SAYADI
THE VEIL

Shahin Sayadi was born and raised in Abadan, Iran; he arrived in
Montreal, Canada wearing shorts and a T-shirt on February 1, 1986
and, notwithstanding the bitter cold, decided to stay. Shahin studied
technical scenography at Dalhousie University and after completing
his studies, he founded Onelight Theatre, based in Halifax, Nova
Scotia, where he remains Artistic Director. Shahin is also the founder and artistic producer of Prismatic, a national organization that
showcases and celebrates the work of Canada's leading Aboriginal
and culturally diverse artists. Shahin is actively involved in local and
national arts organizations, including volunteering on the board of
directors of the Professional Association of Canadian Theatres in
addition to running the Distinct Artistic Practices committee and
participating in PACT's Ideal Agreement Task Force; co-founding
and representing the Ad Hoc Assembly, an organization of Canada's
Aboriginal and culturally diverse theatre companies, and contribut-
ing to the development of the Legacy Centre for the Arts in Halifax.

The Veil is the slightly fictionalized account of the exceptional life
experiences and survival of a Persian princess, Khanoom. It is the
story of one woman's changing perspective of the world, religion,
politics, and relationships, but most importantly, it is about her
changing perspective of herself and her place in the world.

Khanoom is a Persian woman, who, through twists of fate and her perseverance, came to witness, from a unique perspective, many of the political and social changes that shaped the twentieth century. Khanoom is portrayed at many stages in her life, as a child in an insulated environment, to a rebellious youth, and finally to a grown woman who must make a place for herself in a world entirely different from her own. The story is told from Khanoom's perspective.

The Veil is based on the novel *Khanoom (The Lady)* by Masoud Behnoud.

Premiered at Neptune Theatre, Halifax, and Harbourfront Centre, Toronto, in November 2007, produced by Onelight Theatre

• • •

KHANOOM
Come here, love.
Don't blame your mother, Aziz.
Your mother is a weaving of all the women in her life…
She is you… She is all the women we know…
She is us and them… She is all of us.
In times like this, some women, like me, pick up their child and run… As far away as they possibly can…
And others, like your mother, stay and face the situation.

This is your mother, this pomegranate. She is this pomegranate…

Look at it, it's beautiful… It is red… Inside and out.
You grab it… you try to get the sap by pressuring the skin. If you press too hard, it will burst and its blood will show on you.
She's not an apple… Apples bruise, pomegranates bleed.
She is a pomegranate. Tough skin with pearls of blood inside.
And that's what we all want to be.
Not all of us can, but we all wish we could.
Be pomegranates.

I don't want my daughter in jail
And I don't want to see you harmed in this war
But you cannot blame this on your mother.
She's in there giving her blood
So you and others don't have to be pressed too hard.
So you don't have to bleed…
You know, Nanaz… I was nine years old when I was separated from my mother.

For production rights or information on where to obtain full scripts, please contact the following resources:

For C.E. Gatchalian (*Falling in Time*) and Erin Shields (*If We Were Birds*):

Charles Northcote at Core Literary Inc.
140 Wolfrey Ave., Toronto, ON M4K 1L3
P: (416) 466-4929 E: charlesnorthcote@rogers.com

For Anita Majumdar (*Fish Eyes* and *The Misfit*):

Kishwar Iqbal at the Gary Goddard Agency
149 Church St., 2nd floor, Toronto, ON M5B 1Y4
P: (416) 928-0299 E: info@garygoddardagency.com

For Judith Thompson (*Lion in the Streets*):

Rena Zimmerman at Great North Artists Management
350 Dupont St., Toronto, ON M5R 1V9
P: (416) 925-2051 E: renazimmerman@gnaminc.com

For Peter Anderson (*The Blue Horse*), Aaron Bushkowsky (*Soulless*), Lisa Codrington (*The Aftermath*), Chris Craddock (*The Incredible Speediness of Jamie Cavanaugh*), David S. Craig (*Napalm the*

Magnificent: Dancing with the Dark), Ned Dickens (*Seven*), Sky Gilbert (*Will the Real JT Leroy Please Stand Up?*), Wanda R. Graham (*Kill Zone a love story*), Daniel Macdonald (*A History of Breathing*), Mansel Robinson (*Two Rooms*), Anusree Roy (*Letters to my Grandma*), Diana Tso (*Red Snow*), and David Yee (*carried away on the crest of a wave*):

The Playwrights Guild of Canada
401 Richmond St. W., Suite 350, Toronto, ON M5V 3A8
P: (416) 703-0201 E: info@playwrightsguild.ca

For nisha ahuja (*Cycle of a Sari*); Nina Arsenault (*The Silicone Diaries*); Keith Barker (*The Hours That Remain*); Tara Beagan (*Dreary and Izzy*); Dawn Dumont (*Fancydancer*); Waawaate Fobister (*Agokwe*); Ravi Jain, Katrina Bugaj, Troels Hagen Findsen, and Nicolas Billon (*I'm So Close*); Joan M. Kivanda (*Stori ya*); Jason Maghanoy (*Throat*); ahdri zhina mandiela (*who knew grannie: a dub aria*); Tawiah M'Carthy (*Kente Cloth*); Michael Rubenfeld (*My Fellow Creatures*); Shahin Sayadi (*The Veil*); Jon Lachlan Stewart (*Big Shot*); Julie Tepperman (*YICHUD (Seclusion)*); and Gein Wong (*Hiding Words (for you)*):

Playwrights Canada Press
269 Richmond St. W., Suite 202, Toronto, ON M5V 1X1
P: (416) 703-0013 E: info@playwrightscanada.com

For Michael P. Northey (*Cranked*):

Green Thumb Theatre
5522 McKinnon Street, Vancouver, BC V5R 0B6
P: (604) 254-4055 E: info@greenthumb.bc.ca

For Marie Clements (*Tombs of the Vanishing Indian*), David Copelin
(*The Rabbi of Ragged Ass Road*), Don Hannah (*While We're Young*),
Thomas Morgan Jones (*Samuel and Susan*), and Colleen Murphy
(*The December Man (L'homme de décembre)*):

Michael Petrasek at the Talent House
204A St. George St., Toronto, ON M5R 2N5
P: (416) 960-9686 E: michael@talenthouse.ca

Donna-Michelle St. Bernard is a prolific wordslinger, working for change through the arts. Notable works for the stage include *A Man A Fish*, *Salome's Clothes*, and *Gas Girls*. DM is the former general manager of Native Earth Performing Arts and founding artistic director of New Harlem Productions.

© *Denise Grant*

Yvette Nolan is a playwright, dramaturg and director. She has written several plays, including *Annie Mae's Movement*, *The Unplugging*, and *Job's Wife*. Born in Saskatchewan to an Algonquin mother and an Irish immigrant father and raised in Manitoba, Yvette lived in the Yukon and Nova Scotia before moving to Toronto where she served as Artistic Director of Native Earth Performing Arts from 2003 to 2011.